Light in the Heavens

Letter from the General Editor

The Library of Arabic Literature series offers Arabic editions and English translations of significant works of Arabic literature, with an emphasis on the seventh to nineteenth centuries. The Library of Arabic Literature thus includes texts from the pre-Islamic era to the cusp of the modern period, and encompasses a wide range of genres, including poetry, poetics, fiction, religion, philosophy, law, science, history, and historiography.

Books in the series are edited and translated by internationally recognized scholars and are published in parallel-text format with Arabic and English on facing pages, and are also made available as English-only paperbacks.

The Library encourages scholars to produce authoritative, though not necessarily critical, Arabic editions, accompanied by modern, lucid English translations. Its ultimate goal is to introduce the rich, largely untapped Arabic literary heritage to both a general audience of readers as well as to scholars and students.

The Library of Arabic Literature is supported by a grant from the New York University Abu Dhabi Institute and is published by NYU Press.

Philip F. Kennedy
General Editor, Library of Arabic Literature

كتاب الشِّهاب

في الأمثال والمواعظ والآداب

ألف كلمة ومائتا كلمة من حديث
النبيّ صلّى الله عليه وآله وسلّم

للقاضي محمّد بن سلامة القُضاعيّ

LIBRARY OF
المكتبة
ARABIC
العربية
LITERATURE

Light in the Heavens

Sayings of the Prophet Muḥammad

AL-QĀḌĪ AL-QUḌĀʿĪ

Edited and translated by
TAHERA QUTBUDDIN

Volume editor
SHAWKAT TOORAWA

NEW YORK UNIVERSITY PRESS
New York

NEW YORK UNIVERSITY PRESS
New York

Library of Congress Cataloging-in-Publication Data

Names: Quda'i, Muhammad ibn Salamah, -1062 author. | Qutbuddin, Tahera editor translator. | Quda'i, Muhammad ibn Salamah, -1062. Shihab. English. | Quda'i, Muhammad ibn Salamah, -1062. Shihab.
Title: A light in the heavens : sayings of the Prophet Muhammad / edited and translated by Tahera Qutbuddin.
Description: New York : New York University Press, 2016. | In English and Arabic. | Includes bibliographical references and index.
Identifiers: LCCN 2016018938| ISBN 9781479871469 (cl : alk. paper) | ISBN 9781479867851 | ISBN 9781479821167
Subjects: LCSH: Hadith--Texts.
Classification: LCC BP135.A2 Q3513 2016 | DDC 297.1/2570521--dc23
LC record available at https://lccn.loc.gov/2016018938

New York University Press books are printed on acid-free paper, and their binding materials are chosen for strength and durability.

Series design by Titus Nemeth.

Typeset in Tasmeem, using DecoType Naskh and Emiri.

Typesetting and digitization by Stuart Brown.

Manufactured in the United States of America
c10 9 8 7 6 5 4 3 2 1

Table of Contents

dedicated with deepest gratitude to
my revered father
ʿālim-i āl-i Muḥammad
al-ʿallāmah al-niḥrīr
al-daʿī l-fāṭimī
Syedna Khuzaima Qutbuddin

Abbreviations

AD	*anno Domini* = Gregorian (Christian) year
AH	*anno Hegirai* = Hijrah (Muslim) year
Ar.	Arabic
c.	century
ca.	*circa* = about, approximately
cf.	*confer* = compare
ch., chs.	chapter, chapters
D	al-Dūmī's commentary on *Kitāb al-Shihāb*
d.	died
ed.	editor, edition, edited by
e.g.	for example
fl.	flourished
fol., fols.	folio, folios
ibid.	*ibidem* = in the same place
lit.	literally
M	al-Marāghī's commentary on *Kitāb al-Shihāb*
MS, MSS	manuscript, manuscripts
N	*Musnad al-Shihāb*, al-Salafī edition
n.d.	no date
n.p.	no place
no.	number
p., pp.	page, pages
Q	Qur'an
R	al-Rāwandī's commentary on *Kitāb al-Shihāb*
r.	ruled
S	al-Sijilmāsī's commentary on *Kitāb al-Shihāb*
sic	*sic erat scriptum* = thus was it written
s.v., s.vv.	*sub verbo, sub voce* = under the word
viz.	*videlicet* = namely
vol., vols.	volume, volumes
Y	anonymous Yemeni commentary on *Kitāb al-Shihāb* dated 554/1159, MS #5

Acknowledgments

Many people helped see this project to completion, and I take this opportunity to express my heartfelt appreciation:

My late father Syedna Khuzaima Qutbuddin, leader of the Dawoodi Bohra Muslim community and a venerable scholar, tutored me on the prophet Muḥammad's hadith regularly since childhood; throughout my work on this book, his blessings, and those of his successor, my brother Syedna Taher Fakhruddin, have been a constant source of encouragement and inspiration. My mother, Sakina Aaisaheba, has always been a font of love, guidance and blessings.

Several scholars and editors helped shape the project. My project editor at LAL, Professor Shawkat Toorawa, spent innumerable hours reviewing each line of the text in great detail; no one could be better skilled in the valences of rendering classical Arabic into lucid English, or kinder. The input of the anonymous executive reviewer was most valuable in helping me with fine-tuning in the final stages. The anonymous peer reviewers' suggestions on the initial sample were thoughtful and I took them to heart. Professor Ahmed El-Shamsy, my colleague at the University of Chicago, answered questions about Hadith. My brothers and sisters—especially Dr. Aziz, and Dr. Bazat-Saifiyah, and also Bazat-Tyebah, Dr. Abde-Ali, Fatema, Arwa-Qurratulain, and Dr. Husain Qutbuddin—all scholars of Arabic in their own right, gave valuable feedback on various parts of the project. My fellow LAL editors—Professors Philip Kennedy, James Montgomery, Joseph Lowry, Julia Bray, Devin Stewart, and Michael Cooperson—generously helped solve some of the text's enigmatic pieces and pitched in with ideas for rendering the title. LAL editorial director Chip Rossetti, associate managing editor Gemma Juan-Simó, and digital production manager Stuart Brown then efficiently shepherded the project to publication, together with the hard work of the indexer, Elias Saba; the copy editor, Allison Brown; and the proofreader, Alia Soliman.

A number of individuals helped acquire manuscripts. I thank Dr. Marlis Saleh, Middle East Librarian at the University of Chicago, for the Chester Beatty manuscript; University of Chicago graduate students Yaşar Tolga Cora, Ipek Hüner-Cora, and Ayse Polat for manuscripts from Istanbul libraries; Professor Bernard Haykel of Princeton University and Sayyid Ahmad Ishaq of the Zaydi Institute in Sanaa for the Yemeni manuscript; Mr. Mohamed Shehata for manuscripts from Cairo's Dār al-Kutub; Dr. Saud al-Sarhan and the King Faisal Center for Research and Islamic Studies, Riyadh, Saudi Arabia, for copies of manuscripts from the Ẓāhiriyyah, Escorial, and Topkapi libraries; and Professor Bilal Orfali of the American University of Beirut for a copy of an edition of *Musnad al-Shihāb*.

My husband Abduz-Zahir Mohyuddin is the best critical sounding board for all my professional activities. And my son Hyder always helps too—his sweet pride in his mother's work warms my heart.

To all, I am sincerely grateful.

جزاكم الله خيرا

Introduction

The prophet Muḥammad (d. 11/632) is regarded by Muslims as God's messenger to humankind. In addition to God's word—the Qur'an—which he conveyed over the course of his life as it was revealed to him, Muḥammad's own words—called hadith—have a very special place in the lives of Muslims. Many of Muḥammad's hadiths explicate the divine message and consequently form a natural companion to the Qur'an. They wield an authority second only to the Book of God and are cited by Muslims as testimonial texts in a wide array of religious, scholarly, and popular literature—such as liturgy, exegesis, jurisprudence, oration, poetry, linguistics, and much more besides. Preachers, politicians, and scholars alike rely on hadith to establish the truth of their positions, and laypeople cite them in conversations in their daily lives. These sayings disclose the ethos of the earliest period of Islam, the culture and society of seventh-century Arabia, and the literary milieu of the time. Since they also form an integral part of the Muslim psyche, they reveal the values and thinking of the medieval and modern Muslim community. Most importantly, they provide a direct window into the inspired vision of one of the most influential humans in history.

Collecting Muḥammad's words was a major preoccupation for scholars through the centuries, resulting in a profusion of compilations. The focus of most compilers was doctrinal and legal. They aimed to collect sayings that would guide the community in its practice, and the larger part of their compilations explicated rules of ritual worship and civic and criminal regulations. What is more, they couched these sayings within the lengthy scholarly apparatus of authentication.

Among these abundant legally grounded and specialist-oriented collections, *Light in the Heavens* (*Kitāb al-Shihāb*), the compilation of the Fatimid chancery official, Egyptian Shāfiʿī judge, and Sunni Hadith scholar al-Qāḍī al-Quḍāʿī (d. 454/1062) stands out. Although its content overlaps with other collections, its overall conceptualization is distinctively pietistic, ethical, and pragmatic. The larger part of the collection's sayings are devoted to encouraging universal human values such as truthfulness, compassion, and courage, and conversely to discouraging immoral behaviors such as deception, arrogance, and oppression. Al-Quḍāʿī was a specialist of Hadith—and considered a trustworthy transmitter by his peers and by later scholars—but he compiled his book for the nonspecialist. Unlike other compilations, *Light in the Heavens* consists mainly of pithy one-liners containing just the hadith text; the authenticating chains of transmission and accompanying reports al-Quḍāʿī placed in a companion scholarly book, *Musnad al-Shihāb* (*The Transmissions of the Shihāb*). The accessibility and wide relevance of *Light in the Heavens* has resulted in its being used for centuries as a teaching text for children as well as adults, and many of its sayings are dearly familiar to individuals of different denominations and ethnicities—whether Shiʿi or Sunni, scholar or layperson, Arab, Persian, Turk, or South Asian.

Prophet Muḥammad: Life, Lessons, and Legacy

Abū l-Qāsim Muḥammad ibn ʿAbd Allāh ibn ʿAbd al-Muṭṭalib, from the prominent clan of Hāshim of the Ḥijāzī tribe of Quraysh, was born in Mecca around AD 570.[1] Located between the two great empires of the Zoroastrian Sassanids in Persia and the Christian Byzantines in Syria, the majority of those living in the arid Arabian Peninsula at this time were pagan and nomadic; some settlements flourished around oases or wells, among them the shrine city of Mecca. Muḥammad's family, believed by Muslims to be descended from the prophet Abraham (Ibrāhīm) through his son Ishmael (Ismāʿīl), served as guardians of the Kaaba, a sacred shrine built by Abraham. According to information preserved in the Muslim record, even in his childhood, Muḥammad stood out among the Meccans, who singled him out with the honorific title "The Trustworthy One." Orphaned in infancy, he was brought up by his grandfather ʿAbd al-Muṭṭalib, then by his uncle Abū Ṭālib, whom he accompanied on trade expeditions to Syria.

At twenty-five, he married Khadījah, a forty-year-old widow for whom he had served as trading agent. He had six children with her: two sons, Qāsim and ʿAbd Allāh, nicknamed al-Ṭayyib and al-Ṭāhir, who both died in infancy, and four daughters, Zaynab, Ruqayyah, Umm Kulthūm, and Fāṭimah, who survived into adulthood. After Khadījah's death, Muḥammad's concubine, an Egyptian Copt named Māriyah, bore him a son, Ibrāhīm, who also died in infancy. Muḥammad's line continued through his youngest daughter, Fāṭimah, who married Abū Ṭālib's son and Muḥammad's ward, ʿAlī. ʿAlī later became the first imam for the Shi'a, and fourth caliph for the Sunnis. In a saying in this collection, Muḥammad says, "My kin are like Noah's Ark—those who climb aboard are saved, those who waver are drowned" (§11.1).

Muḥammad was a thoughtful and quiet man who often went to the mountains outside Mecca to meditate. During one such visit to Mount Ḥirāʾ—at forty years of age, in ca. AD 610—he received what he believed was a revelation from God. The archangel Gabriel appeared before him and said, «Recite in the name of your lord, the creator.»[2] This was the first of many revelations, which would be memorized by believers and later compiled into the codex of the Qurʾan. Muḥammad believed he had been charged as God's messenger (*rasūl Allāh*) and selected as the seal of the prophets, a group which included major biblical figures such as Adam, Noah, Abraham, Moses, and Jesus. With the creed "There is no god but God" (*lā ilāha illā llāh*), he began to call others to the new religion of Islam (literally, "commitment [to God]"). He first approached Khadījah, then ʿAlī, who both accepted Islam, then ʿAlī's brother Jaʿfar. After a few years, he approached other members of Quraysh who were close to him. Abū Bakr was one of the earliest converts and later became Muḥammad's father-in-law; after Muḥammad's death he would become the first Sunni caliph. Muḥammad also preached to the Arabians who came to Mecca for the annual pilgrimage. Slowly the numbers grew.

The revelations of the Meccan period, and Muḥammad's own orations from this time, were doctrinal and apocalyptic, calling to the worship of the one creator; urging humility, pious deeds, accountability for one's actions, and compassion for the disadvantaged; and warning of the imminent hereafter. In a saying in this collection, Muḥammad explains the exhortatory approach of his mission, stating: "I was sent with profound words" (§3.3). Using desert imagery and camel metaphors, these words painted rhythmic, vivid scenes of the delights of paradise and the agonies of hellfire. They elaborated on Muḥammad's miraculous night journey to Jerusalem, and his ascension through the seven heavens to the throne of God, where the five daily prayers were prescribed. They preached kindness to orphans, help to widows, and generosity to the needy. And they condemned idol worship, materialism, and common pagan Arabian practices such as female infanticide and blood vengeance.

Angered by Muḥammad's anti-establishment message, the Meccans began persecuting him and his followers. In AD 615, Muḥammad sent some of his vulnerable followers to Abyssinia across the Red Sea to seek refuge with the

Christian Negus; they later rejoined the Muslims in Medina. In AD 616, the Meccans instituted a social boycott against Muḥammad's clan, demanding they turn him over, but Abū Ṭālib, patriarch of the Hāshim clan, refused; the boycott ended after a few months. In AD 619, both Abū Ṭālib and Khadījah died. Abū Lahab, another of Muḥammad's uncles, became the new leader of the Hāshim, and he deprived Muḥammad and the Muslims of clan protection. With his life in danger, Muḥammad began to look for a safe haven from which to preach his message. He approached the tribe of Thaqīf in Taif, but they refused him shelter. Then in AD 621 a group from the northern oasis of Yathrib came to Mecca for the pilgrimage and accepted Islam. The following year, AD 622, they came back in greater numbers, and invited Muḥammad to make their city his home. After thirteen years of preaching in Mecca, Muḥammad emigrated to Yathrib. The year would be counted as the first of the Hijri Islamic calendar (named for the Hijrah, or emigration), and the city would henceforth be known as the City of the Prophet, in Arabic Madīnat al-Nabī, commonly shortened to Madīnah (Medina).

In the year 1/622, with Muḥammad's arrival in Medina, a new phase began for Islam. Now at the head of a polity, Muḥammad occupied the additional roles of governor, legislator, and military commander. Medina was home to the pagan tribes of Aws and Khazraj, whose majority accepted Islam, and the Jewish tribes of Naḍīr, Qaynuqāʿ, and Qurayẓah, whose majority remained Jewish. These tribes signed a pact of mutual defense and cooperation, designating themselves a unified community who pledged obedience to "God and Muḥammad." The Muslim tribes of Medina came to be known as the Allies, and those who migrated to Medina with Muḥammad or soon thereafter came to be known as the Emigrants. Both groups would be lauded by later Muslims for their service to Islam in its difficult early phase. Collectively, they are known as Muḥammad's companions, about whom he said, "My companions are like stars—those who follow them will be guided" (§11.2).

Muḥammad lived in Medina for the next, and final, ten years of his life.[3] The Quraysh continued to menace him, and there were several military skirmishes between them, as well as larger pitched battles, including Badr, Uḥud, the Trench (or the Confederates), and lastly, the Conquest of Mecca. There were also disagreements within Medina between the Muslim and Jewish tribes. The latter, according to the Muslim sources, had plotted secretly with the Meccans against Muḥammad, and he subsequently expelled two tribes from the city and executed the members of a third. He also fought the Jews of Khaybar, a northward oasis, who had allied with the Meccans against him. Eventually, Muḥammad emerged victorious, and by the end of the tenth year, the larger part of the residents of the Arabian Peninsula had accepted Muḥammad as their prophet.

In these years, Muḥammad prescribed further rites of worship and piety: the annual alms-levy, fasting in the month of Ramadan, and the hajj pilgrimage to Mecca. He exhorted kindness to parents and charity for all. He also legislated on civic affairs and criminal issues, giving rulings which were to become binding precedents. Preaching, guiding, and counselling, Muḥammad promoted consciousness of God, individual and collective piety, a strong moral fiber, social justice, and compassion for all God's creatures.

In 10/632, Muḥammad performed his only hajj to Mecca, what came to be known as "The Farewell Pilgrimage." According to the Shiʿa, he publicly appointed ʿAlī as his successor immediately afterward at a place called Ghadīr Khumm. Upon his return to Medina, Muḥammad fell ill, and a few months later, in the year 11/632, passed away at the age of sixty-three. In just twenty-three years, Muḥammad had integrated pagan Arabia into a dynamic community united under the banner of monotheistic Islam. Within two decades, Muslims would conquer Syria, Iraq, Iran, Egypt, and North Africa. In twenty more years, they would reach Spain in the West and Central Asia and Sind in the East. Over time, with the efforts of teachers, savants, and mystics, Muḥammad's message would spread even further.

Hadith: Transmission, Collection, and Tools of Scholarship

Muḥammad's hadith include his many sermons and speeches, his answers to questions, his verbal responses to life situations, and also his deeds and gestures. There is a correspondingly rich history of hadith transmission and collection. And medieval Muslim scholars and modern academics have developed an extensive set of critical tools for their assessment.

Muḥammad lived in an oral milieu where writing was limited to important documents, and literary production was overwhelmingly that of the spoken word. The Qur'an describes him as "*ummī*," which according to some interpretations means "unlettered." Other understandings differ,[4] but whether Muḥammad was lettered or not, his words are the product of his oral milieu, and their orality is intrinsic to any discussion of their style and authenticity. The formal verbal productions of primarily oral communities are rooted in mnemonics-based aesthetics. They are permeated with stylistic devices that are a physiological aid to memorization. Like the Qur'an, and similar to orations and proverbs by others from this period, Muḥammad's sayings are condensed, rhythmic, and visual. These rhetorical features—combined with the attested powerful memories of oral societies and the early Muslims' compelling motivation to preserve the words of their adored prophet—ensured the continuity of Muḥammad's teachings.

Muḥammad's sayings were transmitted orally for about a 150 years, relayed by word of mouth over several generations. Early transmitters narrated hadiths in divergent modes: Muḥammad's deeds and gestures were transmitted in their gist, while his words were transmitted partly in their gist and partly verbatim, in a mode in between the meaning-based transmission of historical reports and the verbatim transmission of the Qur'an and poetry. Muḥammad's family and close companions were the first narrators. The subsequent generation of Muslims, known as "followers," and the generation after them, called "followers of the followers," continued the work of preservation. Among these early hadith transmitters, we find master narrators who regularly taught hadith in the urban centers of Islam.

Over the century and a half of primarily oral transmission, we see a steady increase of concurrent written transcription. A fraction of Muḥammad's words was written down during his lifetime and immediately after, in written collections of hadith called *ṣaḥīfah*.[5] In the generation following, notebooks of hadith made their appearance. These notebooks were used as aide-mémoire, and master narrators from the followers and followers' followers are reported to have transcribed hadith into such notebooks for use in their teaching sessions. Although some of the early Muslims were against writing hadith for fear they may be confused with the text of the Qur'an, there were others who deemed it beneficial and they cited Muḥammad himself encouraging the practice.

Following the introduction of paper from China in ca. 132/750 and the corresponding burgeoning of writing in the third/eighth and fourth/ninth centuries, hadith (and other early verbal materials) were systematically transcribed in written books. Over the following centuries, some of these hadith collections attained canonical status. For Sunnis, the "six books"—of al-Bukhārī (d. 256/870), Muslim (d. 261/875), Abū Dā'ūd (d. 275/888), al-Tirmidhī (d. 279/892), al-Nasā'ī (d. 303/915), and the sixth either Ibn Mājah (d. 273/887) or, depending on the listing, Mālik (d. 179/796)—are trusted compilations. Two popular collections were put together by al-Nawawī (d. 676/1277, both translated into English).[6] Al-Quḍāʿī's *Light in the Heavens* was another text with substantial currency. For the Twelver Shiʿa, trusted compilations are those by al-Kulaynī (d. 329/940) and Ibn Bābūyah (d. 381/991), and two by al-Ṭūsī (d. 672/1273), together known as the "four books." For the Fatimid-Ismāʿīlī Shiʿa, the hadith citations of al-Qāḍī al-Nuʿmān (d. 363/974) are authoritative: *Sharḥ al-akhbār* for historical and doctrinal material, and *Daʿāʾim al-Islām* for legal hadith. A significant Zaydī Shiʿi work is *Musnad al-Imām Zayd*, attributed to Zayd ibn ʿAlī Zayn al-ʿĀbidīn (d. 122/740). There is some overlap in the contents of the Sunni and Shiʿi collections, but there are also distinct differences.

Of the tens of thousands of sayings that have come down to us, a good number are likely genuine. But erroneous transmission, inaccurate copying, and deliberate fabrication to further sectarian or political agendas gave rise to a profusion of materials in which the chaff became mixed with the grain. Muslim scholars developed a complex set of tools and terms to assess a hadith's authenticity. One of the tools considered most effective by Sunni scholars was assessment of a hadith's "chain of transmission" (*isnād*), that is, the reliability of the sequence of narrators and the trustworthiness of each narrator.[7] The stronger the chain of transmission, the stronger the probability was of a saying being genuine. They categorize the material on the basis of this probability as sound, good, weak, and a few in-between categories. The Shiʿa, in contrast, deem long *isnād*s and accompanying biographical verifications unnecessary and even misleading: as long as an imam or his appointee has attested to the genuineness of a hadith, it is considered authentic.[8] Western scholarship on Hadith has proliferated since the late nineteenth century—the earliest works focused on "Hadith criticism," while more recent works have inspected its myriad aspects.[9] Modern Western scholars do not, however, appear to have written about *Light in the Heavens*.

Al-Qāḍī al-Quḍāʿī (d. 454/1062): Career and Books

The compiler of *Light in the Heavens*, al-Qāḍī al-Quḍāʿī, was a jurist of the Sunni-Shāfiʿī school of legal thought, and an eminent scholar of Hadith and history who flourished in Fatimid Cairo. His full name was Abū ʿAbd Allāh Muḥammad ibn Salāmah ibn Jaʿfar ibn ʿAlī ibn Ḥakmūn al-Quḍāʿī (thus an affiliate of the clan of Quḍāʿah from the tribe of Ḥimyar). The biographical sources refer to him most frequently as "judge of Egypt" and "compiler of *Light in the Heavens*."[10]

A senior government official for the Shiʿi Fatimids, al-Quḍāʿī performed several singular functions for them. He was judge over their Sunni subjects; he traveled in 447/1055 to Constantinople as Fatimid emissary to the Byzantine court;[11] and he served (indirectly) in their chancery, being scribe for a time for the vizier ʿAlī ibn Aḥmad al-Jarjarāʾī (d. 436/1045). Although the sources do not mention specific interactions, al-Quḍāʿī would presumably have had contact with the eminent Fatimid scholar al-Muʾayyad al-Shīrāzī (d. 470/1078), who was head of the chancery from 443/1051 to 448/1056.

Al-Quḍāʿī's scholarship was highly respected, especially in the collection and transmission of hadith. Sunni scholars deemed al-Quḍāʿī to be a "trustworthy" (*thiqah*) transmitter of hadith. His student Ibn Mākūlā (d. 475/1082) praised him, saying: "He has mastered many different sciences . . . I know none in Egypt who approach his stature."[12] Writing a century later, the jurist al-Silafī (d. 576/1180) said of him: "His fame absolves me from lengthy expositions . . . he is counted among the trustworthy and reliable transmitters."[13] An indication of al-Quḍāʿī's eminence in the field of Hadith scholarship is the fact that he is cited in the chains of transmission of numerous well-regarded compilations.

Following Ibn Mākūlā and al-Silafī, several prominent medieval biographers chronicled al-Quḍāʿī's career and writings.[14] They tell us that al-Quḍāʿī heard and transmitted hadith in his homeland of Egypt, as well as during his travels in Syria en route to Constantinople, in Constantinople, and in Mecca and Medina, where he performed the hajj in 445/1053. They record the names of his teachers, including several distinguished scholars.[15] And they tell us about his students, saying he transmitted hadith to men who would become well-known jurists in their own right.[16] One student, Muḥammad ibn Abī Naṣr al-Ḥumaydī (d. ca. 450/1058), declared that the "*Shihāb* turned me into a *shihāb*," that is, a star.[17]

Al-Quḍāʿī produced thirteen[18] major books on a wide range of subjects.[19] Five are extant, namely:

1. *Light in the Heavens: Sayings of the Prophet Muḥammad* (*Kitāb al-Shihāb fī l-amthāl wa-l-mawāʿiẓ wa-l-ādāb: alf kalimah wa-miʾatā kalimah min ḥadith al-nabī ṣallā-llāhu ʿalayhi wa-ālihī wa-sallam*, lit. Book of the blazing star containing aphorisms, counsels, and directions for refined behavior: 1,200 maxims from the hadith of the prophet). It has been published in several trade editions.

2. *The Transmissions of Light in the Heavens* (*Musnad al-Shihāb*), companion volume to *Light in the Heavens*, containing full chains of transmission and contextual anecdotes, published in two editions.
3. *A Treasury of Virtues: Sayings, Sermons and Teachings of ʿAlī* (*Dustūr maʿālim al-ḥikam wa-maʾthūr makārim al-shiyam min kalām amīr al-muʾminīn ʿAlī ibn Abī Ṭālib*, lit. A compendium of signposts of wisdom and a documentation of qualities of virtue from the words of the commander of the faithful ʿAlī ibn Abī Ṭālib), a collection of "words and eloquent sayings, wise maxims and counsels, directions for refined behavior, answers to questions, prayers and communions with God, and preserved verse and allegories" ascribed to Imam ʿAlī ibn Abī Ṭālib. It is a companion volume to *Light in the Heavens*, published in several editions, including a Library of Arabic Literature edition and translation.
4. *The Book of Reports about the Prophets, the History of the Caliphs, and the Rule of the Princes* (*Kitāb al-Inbāʾ ʿan al-anbiyāʾ wa-tawārīkh al-khulafāʾ wa-wilāyat al-umarāʾ*), also called *Al-Quḍāʿī's History: From the Creation of Adam to the Year 427 [1036]* (*Tārīkh al-Quḍāʿī: min khalq Ādam ḥattā sanat 427 AH*), and also called *Springs of Information and Branches of Reports about the Caliphs* (*ʿUyūn al-maʿārif wa-funūn akhbār al-khalāʾif*), a book on the history of the prophets and caliphs up to the reign of the Fatimid imam-caliph al-Ẓāhir. It has been published in several editions.
5. *Details of Reports and Gardens of Lessons* (*Daqāʾiq al-akhbār wa-ḥadāʾiq al-iʿtibār*), a work of wisdom sayings, published in 1883.[20]

The following eight works are lost:

1. *Institutions of Egypt* (*Kitāb Khiṭaṭ Miṣr*), also known as *Selected Reports of Institutions and Vestiges* (*Al-Mukhtār fī dhikr al-khiṭaṭ wa-l-āthār*), a book on the history of Egypt ascribed to al-Quḍāʿī by Yāqūt al-Ḥamawī (d. 626/1229), Ibn Khallikān (d. 681/1282), al-Maqrīzī (d. 845/1441), al-Qalqashandī (d. 820/1418), and Ibn Taghrī-Birdī (d. 874/1469), all of whom cite material from it.[21]
2. *Qurʾan Commentary* (*Tafsīr*), in twenty volumes according to the modern scholar al-Ziriklī, first mentioned by al-Silafī, then by al-Maqrīzī, and cited by al-Qalqashandī.[22]
3. *The Merits of al-Shāfiʿī* (*Kitāb Manāqib al-Imām al-Shāfiʿī*), or *The Book of Reports about al-Shāfiʿī* (*Kitāb Akhbār al-Shāfiʿī*), a hagiographical

work on the merits of the founder of al-Quḍāʿī's legal school, ascribed to him by Ibn ʿAsākir (d. 571/1176).[23]

4. *Compendium of Teachers* (*Muʿjam al-shuyūkh*), a biographical listing of the scholars from whom al-Quḍāʿī transmitted hadith, ascribed to him by Ibn ʿAsākir.[24]
5. *Book of Numbers* (*Kitāb al-ʿAdad*), ascribed to him by Ibn ʿAṭiyyah (d. 541/1147) and Ibn Bashkuwāl (d. 578/1183).[25]
6. *Book of Beneficial Words* (*Kitāb al-Fawāʾid*), perhaps also on hadith, ascribed to him by Ibn Bashkuwāl.[26]
7. *The Preacher's Pearl and the Worshipper's Treasure* (*Durrat al-wāʿiẓīn wa-dhukhr al-ʿābidīn*), a work on preaching, ascribed to him by Ḥājjī Khalīfah (d. 1067/1657).[27]
8. Ibn Mākūlā's notes from al-Quḍāʿī's lectures, ascribed to him by al-Silafī.[28]

Other titles that editors of al-Quḍāʿī's various works have ascribed to him are variant titles of his *History*, which they list incorrectly as independent works.

Light in the Heavens

The full title of *Light in the Heavens* is—in rhyming Arabic—*Kitāb al-Shihāb fī l-amthāl wa-l-mawāʿiẓ wa-l-ādāb: alf kalimah wa-miʾatā kalimah min ḥadīth al-nabī ṣallā -llāhu ʿalayhi wa-ālihī wa-sallam*. It translates literally as "Book of the blazing star containing aphorisms, counsels, and directions for refined behavior: 1,200 maxims from the hadith of the prophet." In some manuscripts, the work is titled *Shihāb al-akhbār*, "The blazing reports-star," or *Al-Shihāb fī l-ḥikam al-nabawiyyah*, "The blazing star containing the wise sayings of the prophet," or *Al-Shihāb al-nabawī*, "The prophet's blazing star." It is usually mentioned by its shortened title, *Al-Shihāb*—"blazing comet," "shining star," or "luminous planet";[29] the rendering as *Light in the Heavens* is an attempt to capture these various meanings in English.

The book overlaps to some degree with other well-known hadith collections. For each hadith cited in *Light in the Heavens*, the commentator al-Marāghi and the editors of *The Transmissions* list additional sources, which include the major Sunni collections of Ibn Ḥanbal, al-Bukhārī, Muslim, al-Tirmidhī, Abū Dāʾūd, Ibn al-Jawzī, and Ibn Ḥajar al-ʿAsqalānī; many of the *Shihāb*'s hadith are also found in Shiʿi works, such as the collections of al-Qāḍī al-Nuʿmān and al-Ṭūsī.

System and Substance

As a popular collection of the prophet Muḥammad's sayings for the general reader, the system and substance of *Light in the Heavens*' material are straightforward and accessible. In the introduction, al-Quḍāʿī tells us that he has arranged the sayings "uninterruptedly, one following the other, omitting the chains of transmission," which he provides separately in the companion specialist book *The Transmissions*. "For simplified access and ease of memorization," he continues, he has divided the sayings into seventeen "chapters based on similarity of lexical pattern," for example, "Whosoever does X gets Y" and "Do X and you will get Y." This is a relatively unusual method of organization for hadith compilations, but one routinely used in collections of classical Arabic proverbs and sayings—and *Light in the Heavens* contains largely aphoristic material.

The contents of the work are listed by al-Quḍāʿī in his introduction as "testaments, directions for refined behavior, counsels, and maxims" as well as "supplications attributed to the prophet in prayer." Most are succinct one-liners extracted from longer texts of the prophet's sermons and speeches, from answers to questions, from responses to real-life situations, and from anecdotes about his deeds and gestures. Contextual material is provided in *The Transmissions*, in commentaries of *Light in the Heavens*, in other hadith compilations and their commentaries, in biographical works on Muḥammad, and in historical works on early Islam.

Muḥammad's words collected in *Light in the Heavens* preach humane behavior and consciousness of God, and urge the reader to prepare for the imminent hereafter.[30] They counsel repentance of sins and renunciation of worldly matters, and advocate virtuous action. They offer practical advice on daily life issues, keen observations on human nature, and legal rulings on social and economic issues. In one chapter, they quote God directly speaking to humans. The themes, whether worldly or sublime, are couched within an Islamic pietistic framework, consonant with the teachings of the Qur'an.

Imagery is based on flora and fauna from the Arabian Peninsula, as well as cosmic and mundane objects and acts that reflect the lifestyle of the residents of early Islamic Mecca and Medina; numerous sayings also reference them literally. Camels, horses, sheep, dates, turbans, musk, vinegar, salt are all to be found, as are the blacksmith and the perfume vendor. Advice on detailed aspects of everyday life abound: "never skip dinner," "pay a worker his wages," and "wear white garments."

Doctrines and practices of Islam are also abundantly described: the mandatory rites of the daily prayer, the annual alms-levy, fasting, the hajj pilgrimage, and regular and melodious recitation of the Qur'an. Prophets are held up as exemplars. Exhortations to revere and be guided by Muḥammad's progeny, his pious companions, and the learned among the community pepper the collection.

The vast majority of the collection's sayings are devoted to promoting upright character: honesty, integrity, affection, compassion, contentment, scrupulosity, gentleness, harmony, modesty, courage, generosity, fortitude, gratitude, justice, simplicity, trustworthiness, moderation, and forgiveness, as well as giving in charity and seeking counsel. The traits and acts warned against include deception, untruthfulness, harshness, obscenity, drink, fornication, arrogance, aggression, hypocrisy, conceit, begging, and flattery. A large number of sayings advocate the seeking of knowledge and the cherishing of wisdom, and encourage the related traits and acts of careful planning, intellectual curiosity, and asking good questions.

Reception and Renown

Light in the Heavens is al-Quḍāʿī's most celebrated work.[31] Its approachable format and humane content made it popular almost immediately after it was compiled, and the numerous extant manuscripts and their varied places of origin suggest the book's dissemination across the expanse of the Islamic world—from Spain in the West, through North Africa, Egypt, Turkey, Palestine, Syria, and Yemen, to India in the East. Al-Silafī and Ibn ʿAsākir note its prominence in their biographies of al-Quḍāʿī, saying the collection "has spread to the corners of the earth, becoming as clearly visible in the firmament as the blazing star after which it is named."[32]

I have identified sixty-eight commentaries and related works on *Light in the Heavens*, written in Arabic or Persian, with one in Turkish, in both medieval and modern times (see details of extant works in the bibliography).[33]

Fifty-five of these are medieval works, dating from the late fifth/eleventh century through the twelfth/eighteenth century, and ranging widely in the authors' places of work and faith denominations. They include:

- twenty-four Arabic commentaries—including extant ones by Ibn Waḥshī (d. 502/1109), al-Nasafī (d. 537/1142), al-Rāwandī (d. 537/1142), one anonymous (d. 554/1159), two by al-Sijilmāsī (fl. 7th/13th c.), Ibn al-Warrāq (n.d.), and Bābī (n.d.), and a lost commentary by the famed litterateur Ḍiyā' al-Dīn Ibn al-Athīr (d. 636/1239);

- twenty-four Arabic response books that assess its *isnāds* (*takhrīj*), or offer an alphabetical rearrangement of its sayings (*tartīb*) or a supplement to it (*takmilah*), or use it as a model for their own hadith works—including extant ones by Ibn Shīrawayh (d. 509/1115), al-Uqlīshī (d. 550/1155), al-Qalʿī (d. 629/1232), Abū l-Saʿādāt (d. 634/1237), al-Ṣāghānī (d. 650/1252), al-ʿIrāqī (d. 806/1403), and al-Munāwī (d. 1030/1621), and a lost work by the well-known scholar al-Suyūṭī (d. 911/1505);
- seven Persian translations with commentaries—including extant ones by Ibn al-Quḍāʿī (fl. ca. 5th/11th c.), Zakī (d. before 567/1171), one anonymous (fl. 8th/14th c.), and Baḥrānī (fl. 10th/16th c.).

In modern times, a total of thirteen related works have been published:

- four Arabic commentaries on *Light in the Heavens* by al-Kattānī, al-Marāghī, al-Dūmī, and Dīsī;
- seven Arabic response works, one each by al-Kattānī (again), al-ʿAzzūzī, and al-Ḥujūjī, and four by al-Ghumārī;
- a translation into Persian by Farkhiyān, and one in French by Khawam; a third is underway in three languages simultaneously, English, Urdu, and Gujarati.[34]

The varied denominational affiliations of the scholars who copied the work and studied it—as noted in the texts of the manuscript and in certificates of study jotted on them—reveals a broad interest across sectarian lines: Shiʿi scholars from all three major groups, Fatimid-Ismāʿīlī, Twelver, and Zaydī, studied the work as assiduously as Sunni scholars of all four major legal schools, Shāfiʿī (which was al-Quḍāʿī's own), Mālikī, Ḥanafī, and Ḥanbalī, as well as of the lesser-known Ẓāhirī school.

Light in the Heavens played an important role in traditional Muslim education, particularly for young children and nonspecialists, but also for scholars, and it appears to have been a regularly featured text in madrasa curricula. For more advanced students of jurisprudence, a commentary seems to have been studied, particularly those of the Sunni Mālikī al-Sijilmāsī and the Twelver Shiʿi al-Rāwandī. The hadith specialists paid special attention to *The Transmissions*. The large number of manuscripts of *Light in the Heavens* and *The Transmissions*, and the numerous study certificates, colophons, commentaries, and *isnād*-assessments, also indicate that these were teaching texts read in numerous study circles in Egypt and elsewhere in the Islamic world.

Light in the Heavens was popular across the far reaches of the Islamic world, being studied by Hadith scholars in North Africa and Spain in the West, as well as Mecca in the center, and Iraq and Iran in the East. In Morocco under the Almohad dynasty (r. 514-667/1121-1269), the *Shihāb* was among the hadith works prescribed for study.[35] Under the Marīnids (r. 642-869/1244-1465), the text's fame continued to grow: Ibn ʿAbbād al-Rundī (d. 792/1390), the famous Mālikī Hadith scholar and Sufi shaykh who flourished in their realms, had memorized *Light in the Heavens* in its entirety.[36] Among the several hundred scholars who are named in the sources as having studied *Light in the Heavens* and *The Transmissions*—often with students of al-Quḍāʿī, or students' students—several are from Spain, from cities such as Toledo, Seville, Granada, Almeria, Mallorca, and Valencia.[37] Additionally, twenty-four scholars with connections to Iran (notably Qazvin) are identified by al-Rāfiʿī (d. 623/1226) as having studied and taught the *Shihāb*.[38] In Baghdad, the famous Ḥanbalī jurist, Hadith scholar, historian, and preacher Ibn al-Jawzī (d. 597/1200) is reported to have transmitted *Light in the Heavens*.[39] In Cairo, it was taught to public audiences by al-Quḍāʿī and his students in the sixth/thirteenth century; three centuries later, the renowned Shāfiʿī Hadith scholar, judge, and historian Ibn Ḥajar al-ʿAsqalānī (d. 852/1449) also taught *The Transmissions* in Cairo to a scholar from the al-Azhar teaching establishment.[40]

Ironically, an indication of the *Shihāb*'s fame comes from the mouth of a detractor, al-Ḥasan ibn Muḥammad al-Ṣāghānī (d. 650/1252), a native of Lahore (in present-day Pakistan), who traveled across the Islamic world, and studied and taught in Ghazna, Mecca, Baghdad, and Delhi. In the introduction to his hadith compilation *Mashāriq al-anwār* (*Rising-places of Celestial Lights*), in which he combined the "sound" hadith collections of al-Bukhārī and Muslim, he lamented that people of his age studied hadith only from al-Uqlīshī's *Al-Najm* (*The Star*), al-Nawawī's *Forty Hadiths*, and from the "books of al-Quḍāʿī," all collections that, according to him, mixed sound hadiths with weak ones.[41] This, he said, is what led him to compile his own, more rigorous work. But he does not reject the *Shihāb* outright; in fact, he writes that he has included its sound sayings in his compilation.[42]

It is fitting to conclude with the views of one medieval scholar and one modern savant, one a Sunni and one Shiʿi. The celebrated literary theorist Ḍiyāʾ al-Dīn

Ibn al-Athīr (d. 636/1239), in his work titled *The Popular Aphorism* (*Al-Mathal al-sāʾir*), advised aspiring chancery scribes to begin their study of hadith with al-Quḍāʿī's *Light in the Heavens*. Ibn al-Athīr was born in Turkey, and he lived in Damascus, where he served as vizier for Saladin and al-Malik al-Afḍal, and then in Mosul, where he was head of the chancery for the last Zangid ruler. He says:

> The first [book] you should memorize of [prophetic] reports is *Light in the Heavens*. It is a short book, and all that is in it may be used, for it contains words of wisdom and manners. Once you have memorized it and are familiar with using it, as I have shown you here, you will have the capacity to deal with, and know, what [kinds of hadith] may be used and what may not. At that time, you can go on to study the *Ṣaḥīḥ* works of al-Bukhārī and Muslim, [Mālik's] *Muwaṭṭaʾ*, [the work of] al-Tirmidhī, the *Sunan* of al-Nasāʾī, and other works of hadith.[43]

More recently, Sayyidnā Ṭāhir Sayf al-Dīn (d. 1385/1965)—fifty-first *dāʿī* of the Ṭayyibī Fatimid-Ismāʿīlīs, and a learned scholar and prolific author and poet from Surat in India—cites a large number of *Shihāb* hadith in his *Treasures of the Imam of the Pious* (*Khazāʾin imām al-muttaqīn*). In his preface to the selection, he echoes the language of al-Quḍāʿī's introduction describing Muḥammad's sayings, and entreats his readers to study them as follows:

> Let us profit from this selection [of sayings] come to us from a prophet fortified with profound words and marvelous sayings. They shine in the sky of that [divine] knowledge which gives benefit in this world and the hereafter—as shining stars lighting up black darkness. For they derive from God's command, written in the Tablet by the Pen.[44]

A Note on the Text

This is the first critical edition of al-Quḍāʿī's (d. 454/1062) *Kitāb al-Shihāb*. It relies on several early and valuable manuscripts, many used for the first time in modern scholarship.

Because *Kitāb al-Shihāb* became popular as a teaching text from the time of its first dissemination, an extraordinarily large number of valuable manuscripts survive. Also extant are several important manuscripts of the companion volume, *Musnad al-Shihāb*, which contains the chains of transmission for the *Shihāb*'s hadiths, and some early manuscripts of commentaries that include, cite, and comment on them.[45] There is hardly a major manuscript library in the world that does not own multiple copies of *Kitāb al-Shihāb* and its companion texts.

Primary Manuscripts Used in This Edition

In this edition, I rely primarily on four Egyptian manuscripts deriving directly from al-Quḍāʿī's original autograph or from those used by his students in their study with him. The following are the primary manuscripts in chronological order:

1. [ظ] Egyptian manuscript of *Musnad al-Shihāb* dated 449/1057, located in the Dār al-Kutub al-Ẓāhiriyyah in Damascus, catalog number Hadith 359. It was copied by an anonymous student of al-Quḍāʿī who read it with al-Quḍāʿī himself in the al-ʿAtīq (ʿAmr) Mosque in Fustat.[46] This manuscript is approximately four-fifths complete.[47] It contains eighty-six folios, divided into seven parts (*juz'*, pl. *ajzā'*).[48] Presumably bound with one or more additional texts that go up to folio 133, the *Musnad al-Shihāb* begins at folio 134 and goes to 220, with some gaps. Written in an unvocalized, mostly undotted, and cramped *naskh* script, it is readable with difficulty.
2. [ا] Egyptian manuscript of *Musnad al-Shihāb* dated 453/1061, located in the Escorial Library in Madrid, catalog number Derenbourg [D] 752, Casiri [C] 748. It was copied under al-Quḍāʿī's dictation and read with him in Fustat the year before his death by a student named Jumāhir ibn

ʿAbd al-Raḥmān ibn Jumāhir al-Mālikī l-Andalusī.[49] This is a partial manuscript, approximately a quarter of the whole, with thirty-four folios.[50] The chains of transmission (*isnād*s) are written in casual Maghribī script, with the interspersed hadith texts written out more distinctively. The manuscript contains emendations in the margins. Some parts are smudged from water damage. It contains no vocalization, almost no dotting, and the text—especially the *isnād*s—are readable only with considerable difficulty.

3. [ك and ت] Egyptian manuscript containing both *Kitāb al-Shihāb* [ك] and *Musnad al-Shihāb* [ت], from the 6th/12th century, located in the Topkapi Palace Museum Library in Istanbul, catalog number Aḥmad III Hadith 370.[51] This is the earliest extant manuscript of the stand-alone *Kitāb al-Shihāb*, and also the earliest full manuscript of *Musnad al-Shihāb*, and is thus a very valuable source. Most importantly, it has a short and distinguished lineage connecting it directly to al-Quḍāʿī: It was copied by a scholar named Ḥasan ibn ʿAbd al-Bāqī l-Madīnī (d. 598/1201) from the manuscript of one of al-Quḍāʿī's students, the eminent Sufi shaykh and Arabic philologist Muḥammad ibn Barakāt (d. 520/1126), who copied it in 489/1096 from al-Quḍāʿī's original autograph copy. Moreover, the copyist was himself al-Quḍāʿī's student's student, having obtained a certificate (*ijāzah*) to transmit *Musnad al-Shihāb* from the renowned chancery official Hibat Allāh ibn ʿAlī al-Būṣīrī (d. 598/1201), who obtained his certificate from Ibn Barakāt, who obtained his from al-Quḍāʿī. The manuscript contains a large number of colophons recording further study notices scattered on the margins and between sections throughout. It also contains a large number of comments, corrections, and further *isnād* notices in the margins, in different hands, some of them directly quoting al-Quḍāʿī. The manuscript is complete in 191 folios. It is written in clear, adequately spaced *naskh* script, and is fully dotted and vocalized. Folios 1–168 contain *Musnad al-Shihāb*, and folios 168–191 contain *Kitāb al-Shihāb*.
4. [م] Egyptian manuscript of *Musnad al-Shihāb* from the 6th/12th century, located in the Dār al-Kutub al-Miṣriyyah in Cairo, catalog number Hadith 452.[52] This is a companion manuscript to MS [ت], with the same pedigree, thus apparently read in the same study sessions: it was written by an anonymous copyist, who read the text with al-Būṣīrī, who read it in 517/1123 in Fustat with Ibn Barakāt, who read it with al-Quḍāʿī.[53]

The beginning and end of each of its ten parts contain study notices by notable scholars.[54] The manuscript also contains comments, corrections, and further *isnād* notices in the margins in different hands. The manuscript is complete, in 499 folios, with just a few folios missing or blotted out.[55] It is written in a cursory but relatively clear *naskh* script, though unvocalized and mostly undotted.

Supplementary Manuscripts Used in This Edition

For comparative purposes, I have used the following eight early manuscripts from the 6th/12th to the 9th/15th centuries copied in several parts of the Islamic world, including Egypt, Yemen, Palestine, Spain, and North Africa (listed in chronological order):[56]

1. Yemeni Zaydī manuscript of an anonymous commentary, *Sharḥ al-Shihāb*, dated 554/1159, located in the Grand Mosque (Jāmiʿ Kabīr) in Sanaa, part of the *waqf* collection of al-Khizānah al-Mutawakkiliyyah, catalog number 491/1167.[57] The manuscript is written in cramped *naskh* script, readable with difficulty. It uses archaic orthography (e.g., صلوة and تطفي), with dots frequently missing and minimal vocalization, and features marginal corrections in the same hand. The text is well preserved and shows no lacunae; it adds seven hadiths not in the other manuscripts.[58] The manuscript is in 238 folios; the first 227 comprise *Sharḥ al-Shihāb*, and the final 11 comprise two Zaydī jurisprudential texts. The commentary within this manuscript is denoted by Y in the endnotes.
2. Andalusian manuscript of *Musnad al-Shihāb* from ca. 6th/12th century, located in the Dār al-Kutub al-Ẓāhiriyyah in Damascus, catalog number Hadith 538.[59] The name of the copyist is not mentioned, but Murcia in Spain is noted as its place of completion. This is an almost complete manuscript of 122 folios, divided in ten parts, with only the first hundred hadiths missing. It is written in stylized Maghribī script, somewhat cramped and readable with difficulty, and is dotted with some vocalization. It contains some emendations and extra *isnād*s in the margins.[60]
3. Maghribī manuscript of *Kitāb al-Shihāb* dated 598/1201, located in the Süleymaniye Library in Istanbul, catalog number 34 Sü-Aşir 69.[61] The manuscript is complete in 62 folios, written in handsome Maghribī calligraphy, fully vocalized, with gold illumination and gold rondelles

between maxims and parallel clauses. It is well preserved and has no lacunae, but a few sections are smudged and hard to read. This manuscript was used and corrected by scholars over the centuries, and includes in its margins numerous emendations, variants, and lexical and other interpretations written in different hands. It also contains the ownership marks of Muḥammad ibn Sulaymān (d. 1143/1730), a North African Mālikī Hadith scholar.

4. Manuscript of *Sharḥ al-Shihāb* dated 708/1308, located in the library of Princeton University, catalog number Islamic Manuscripts, Garrett no. 707H. The commentary's full title is given as *Sharḥ Shihāb al-akhbār fī l-ḥikam wa-l-amthāl wa-l-ādāb min al-aḥādīth al-nabawiyyah.* Comprising twelve chapters, the manuscript is complete in 70 folios. It is written in clear *naskh* script and is fully dotted and partially vocalized. The names of the commentary's author and of various owners of the manuscript appear to have been deliberately erased or blotted out.
5. Manuscript of *Kitāb al-Shihāb* dated 735/1335, located in the Chester Beatty Library in Dublin, catalog number 4433. No copyist name or place name is given. It is nearly complete, written in clear *naskh* script, fully dotted, and nearly wholly vocalized.[62] The full manuscript is 145 folios, of which *Kitāb al-Shihāb* comprises the first 31. It is followed by an anonymous *Sharḥ al-Shihāb*, and a hadith collection by al-Ḥasan ibn ʿArafah al-ʿAbdī (d. 257/871).
6. North African manuscript of *Kitāb al-Shihāb* dated 798/1396, located in the Chester Beatty Library in Dublin, catalog number 5182. The manuscript is almost complete in 51 folios, written in large, handsome Maghribī calligraphy, fully vocalized, with gold illumination and gold rondelles between maxims and parallel clauses. The copyist is Abū l-ʿAbbās Aḥmad ibn ʿAlī al-Qabāʾilī;[63] I could locate no place name, but the copyist's geographical affiliation, al-Qabāʾilī, is the name of a tribe active in modern-day Libya and Algeria.[64]
7. Palestinian manuscript of *Kitāb al-Shihāb* dated 877/1473, located in the Chester Beatty Library in Dublin, catalog number 3859. The copyist is Shihāb al-Dīn Abū l-Faḍl Aḥmad ibn ʿAbd al-Raḥmān ibn ʿAbd al-Karīm ibn Makkiyyah al-Shāfiʿī l-Nābulusī (d. 907/1502). The full manuscript is in 126 folios, of which *Kitāb al-Shihāb* comprises the first 22; it is followed in this manuscript by three additional short treatises by ʿAlī ibn

Abī Ṭālib (d. 40/661), Majd al-Mulk al-Afḍalī (d. 622/1225), and Ibn Makkiyyah, the manuscript's copyist. The manuscript is written in clear *naskh* script, fully dotted and partially vocalized. A colophon on the final *Shihāb* folio says it has been read and corrected against a valuable and correct manuscript in 879/1475. There are two notices of ownership on the first and last folios, the second dated 1170/1756. The manuscript contains no emendations or marginal additions.

8. Manuscript of *Kitāb al-Shihāb* located in the library of Princeton University, catalog number Islamic MSS, Garrett no. 233Bq. The manuscript appears to have no evidence for dating, but according to Philip Hitti in the Garrett catalog, it dates from the 8th/14th century, and was acquired by Princeton from Beirut, Lebanon, in 1925.[65]

Previous Critical Editions of *The Transmissions, Musnad al-Shihāb*

1. al-Quḍāʿī. *Musnad al-Shihāb*. Edited by Ḥamdī ʿAbd al-Majīd al-Salafī. 2 vols. Beirut: Muʾassasat al-Risālah, 1985.[66]
2. al-Quḍāʿī. *Musnad al-Shihāb*. Edited by Ḥāmid ʿAbd Allāh al-Maḥallawī. Beirut: Dār al-Kutub al-ʿIlmiyyah, 2011.[67]

Previous Critical Editions of Commentaries, *Sharḥ al-Shihāb*

1. al-Rāwandī, Quṭb al-Dīn (d. 573/1178). *Diyāʾ al-shihāb fī Sharḥ Shihāb al-Akhbār*. Edited by Mahdī Sulaymānī l-Ashtiyānī. Qom: Dār al-Ḥadīth, 1431/2010.
2. al-Sijilmāsī,[68] Muḥammad ibn Manṣūr (fl. 7th/13th century). *Sharḥ Shihāb al-Quḍāʿī wa-Sharḥ gharībihī*. 2 vols. Edited by ʿAlī Najmī. Beirut: Dār Ibn Ḥazm, 2010.
3. al-Dūmī, Ibn Badrān al-Ḥanbalī. *Sharḥ Kitāb al-Shihāb fī l-ḥikam wa-l-mawāʿiẓ wa-l-ādāb li-l-Imām al-Quḍāʿī*. Edited by Nūr al-Dīn Ṭālib. 2 vols. Damascus and Beirut: Dār al-Nawādir, 2007.
4. al-Marāghī, Abū l-Wafāʾ Muṣṭafā. *Al-Lubāb fī Sharḥ al-Shihāb*. Cairo: al-Majlis al-Aʿlā li-l-Shuʾūn al-Islāmiyyah, 1970.

This Edition

For this edition, I mostly follow the rendering of the 6th/12th century *Kitāb al-Shihāb* Topkapi Egyptian manuscript [ك], privileging the readings of the text over the margins and marginalia, and checking it against *Musnad al-Shihāb* primary manuscripts [ظ], [ا], [ت], and [م]. In the footnotes, I list all significant variants along with the manuscripts in which they occur. For the sake of concision, I do not list the manuscript reading which has been used in my text. In the handful of places where—presumably due to scribal error—the *Kitāb al-Shihāb* manuscript [ك] differs from all the primary *Musnad al-Shihāb* manuscripts, I cite the *Musnad al-Shihāb* reading in the text, and give the [ك] variant in a footnote. Note that these variants occur most often in the gender, form, or tense of a verb, or in the use of a preposition, and more rarely in a noun or adjective. Overall, the rendering in this cluster of manuscripts is remarkably consonant, and I am confident that this edition, based on these source-proximate manuscripts, is very close to al-Quḍāʿī's original.

The nature of variants in these manuscripts of *Kitāb al-Shihāb* and *Musnad al-Shihāb* is quite unusual, and is based on the special relationship between the two companion texts. For each hadith, the *Musnad al-Shihāb* manuscripts [ظ], [ا], [ت], and [م] provide one or more reports (along with the chain of transmission, *isnād*). The multiple reports frequently present variant readings. Based on these variants, the *Kitāb al-Shihāb* manuscript [ك] often presents two options for a word or phrase in a single hadith; one variant is usually noted in the text of the manuscript and another in the margin with the word "both" (*maʿan*) inscribed above or alongside it. A couple of hadiths are present in one but absent from the other.[69]

Additional features of this edition:

- Of the eight supplementary manuscripts from the 6th–9th/12th–15th centuries, six are of *Kitāb al-Shihāb* and one each is of *Musnad al-Shihāb* and *Sharḥ al-Shihāb*. I footnote supplementary manuscripts collectively in a few places in the edition, especially where *Kitāb al-Shihāb* is wholly different from *Musnad al-Shihāb*. I mostly do not footnote their individual variants.[70]
- The phrase *riwāyah iḍāfiyyah* in the footnotes indicates variants written in the cited MSS *in addition to* (rather than *instead of*) the one cited in the text of my edition.
- In the sequencing of hadiths, I follow the order of the *Kitāb al-Shihāb* manuscript [ك]. To maintain concision, I do not footnote the few differing placements;[71] other than some pattern groupings, the format of *Kitāb*

al-Shihāb is a simple list without any substantial thematic impact on the ordering.

- To make the text easier to navigate, I restart the numbering of hadiths in each chapter. For the most part, I preserve thematically or rhetorically connected multipart sayings as single units. I separate out unconnected parts of single hadith into individually numbered units (these are usually signaled in the Arabic text by an opening *wāw* conjunctive). Additionally, I cluster similarly patterned or similarly themed hadith, and add an extra line space between these clusters.
- Some manuscripts of *Kitāb al-Shihāb*, *Musnad al-Shihāb*, and *Sharḥ al-Shihāb*, and all previous editions of *Musnad al-Shihāb* and *Sharḥ al-Shihāb* provide full—albeit sometimes differing—vocalization. I vocalize only those parts of the text that may not be obvious to an educated reader of classical Arabic.

This Translation

Translating the prophet Muḥammad's hadiths, words revered by Muslims, poses several very real challenges to the translator. They are pithily succinct; they are buttressed by a multitude of contextual narratives, each supporting numerous interpretations; they are anchored in the beautifully cadenced rhythms of early Arabic; they draw on a vivid palette of cosmic and desert imagery; and the words and tempos are often specific to the linguistic milieu of seventh-century Arabia. A translator can only fall short, but I have done my best to produce a clear English rendering that preserves the substantive spirit and rhetorical texture of the original words.

Keeping these larger issues in mind—and in keeping with my approach in translating al-Quḍāʿī's collection of ʿAlī ibn Abī Ṭālib's sayings—I strive for sentence-to-sentence translation, rather than word-to-word correspondence, as I find it serves the translation better to convey the essence of what is being said. Where appropriate, I have

- added words to unpack the dense Arabic—but only minimally, preserving any ambiguities in the original;
- modified syntax and morphology for an idiomatic English rendering;
- translated a single Arabic word differently in different places, depending on context;

- used lowercase for pronouns referring to God, and also for several other words commonly rendered in uppercase, such as "the fire" (*al-nār*, i.e., hellfire) and "the garden" (*al-jannah*, i.e., the garden of paradise);
- used my own translations of Qur'anic verses, to maintain consistency and to highlight a given verse's meaning in its context;
- omitted pious invocations attached to the name of God and the prophet Muḥammad (these are preserved in the Arabic); and
- following classical Arabic practice, retained the masculine gender in generic references to humans.

The presence of specialized terminology has been a particular challenge, since certain differences in language arise not just from differences in the signifier words, but more deeply, from differences in the concepts signified. To this end, I have translated selected technical religious terms differently from their conventional English rendering. For example, I often translate "Islam" as "commitment to God" (rather than "submission" to him); *taqwā* as "piety" or "being conscious of God" (rather than "fear of God"); and *zuhd* as "rejection of worldliness" or "indifference to the world" (rather than "rejection of the world" or "asceticism").

MSS Sigla

This alphabetical list of sigla—used to denote the primary manuscripts cited in the edition's footnotes, all of Egyptian provenance—is provided for quick reference; details have been supplied earlier.

ا *Musnad al-Shihāb*, 453/1061, Escorial, Madrid, cat. no. Derenbourg [D] 752, Casiri [C] 748.

ت *Musnad al-Shihāb*, 6th/12th c., Topkapi, Istanbul, cat. no. Aḥmad III Hadith 370.

ظ *Musnad al-Shihāb*, 449/1057, Dār al-Kutub al-Ẓāhiriyyah, Damascus, cat. no. Hadith 359.

ك *Kitāb al-Shihāb*, 6th/12th c., Topkapi, Istanbul, cat. no. Aḥmad III Hadith 370.

م *Musnad al-Shihāb*, 6th/12th c., Dār al Kutub al-Miṣriyyah, Cairo, cat. no. Hadith 452.

Notes to the Introduction

1 The primary sources for Muḥammad's biography include Ma'mar ibn Rāshid, *The Expeditions*; al-Wāqidī, *The Life of Muhammad*; Ibn Isḥāq, *The Life of Muḥammad*; al-Ṭabarī, *The History of al-Ṭabarī*, vols. 6–9; al-Qāḍī al-Nuʿmān, *Sharḥ al-akhbār*. The enormous number of modern studies include Watt, *Muhammad at Mecca* and *Muhammad at Medina*; Hamidullah, *The Life and Work of the Prophet of Islam*; Lings, *Muhammad: His Life Based on the Earliest Sources*; Motzki, ed., *The Biography of Muhammad: The Issue of the Sources*; Rubin, ed., *The Life of Muḥammad*; Schoeler, *The Biography of Muḥammad*; Khalidi, *Images of Muhammad*; Qutbuddin, "Muḥammad"; Fitzpatrick and Walker, eds., *Muhammad in History, Thought, and Culture: An Encyclopedia of the Prophet of God*; Crone, "What Do We Actually Know about Mohammed?"

2 Q ʿAlaq 96:1.

3 In this period, Muḥammad wrote letters to the Sassanid, Byzantine, and Ethiopian rulers inviting them to Islam; see Hamidullah, ed., *Majmūʿat al-wathāʾiq al-siyāsiyyah*.

4 E.g., "*ummī*" is also interpreted as "belonging to the community (*ummah*)" of prophets.

5 Two are extant: *Ṣaḥīfat Hammām ibn Munabbih* and *Ṣaḥīfat ʿAlī ibn Abī Ṭālib*, both edited by Rifʿat Fawzī ʿAbd al-Muṭṭalib, Cairo, 1985–86.

6 Khan, trans., *Gardens of the Righteous*; Cleary, trans., *The Wisdom of the Prophet*; Guezzou, trans., *A Treasury of Hadith*.

7 To help with authentication, a number of secondary genres became important, particularly biographical dictionaries, the earliest of these being Ibn Saʿd's *Great Book of Generations* [of hadith transmitters] (*Al-Ṭabaqāt al-kubrā*).

8 For the Twelver Shiʿa after the death of their eleventh imam in 873/1469 and the immediate occultation of his infant son, the twelfth imam, biographical dictionaries gained increasing relevance, among them *Rijāl* works by al-Ṭūsī and al-Najāshī.

9 Western scholarship on hadith includes works by Goldziher, Schacht, Ṣiddīqī, Kamali, Brown, Motski, and Musa; see details in the bibliography.

10 E.g., al-Dhahabī, *Taʾrīkh al-Islām*, 30:369 and *Siyar aʿlām al-nubalāʾ*, 18:92; Ibn Khallikān, *Wafayāt al-aʿyān*, 4:212; al-Subkī, *Ṭabaqāt al-Shāfiʿiyyah al-kubrā*, 3:62.

11 Ibn al-ʿAdīm (*Bughyat al-ṭalab*, 9:4167) narrates that al-Quḍāʿī was invited to a meal with the Byzantine emperor, who was impressed when he saw him pick up a piece of bread

that had fallen off the table and eat it, honoring the food, as, he said, "has been taught to us by our prophet Muḥammad." The emperor rewarded him handsomely.

12 Ibn Mākūlā, *Kitāb al-Ikmāl*, 7:115.

13 Al-Silafī, *Mashyakhat al-Rāzī*, 1:241–42.

14 Al-Ḥabbāl, *Wafayāt*, 1:87; Ibn ʿAṭiyyah, *Fihrist*, 1:128; al-Samʿānī, *Al-Ansāb*, 4:517; Ibn ʿAsākir, *Taʾrīkh madīnat Dimashq*, 53:167–70; Abū l-Fidāʾ, *Al-Mukhtaṣar*, 2:190; Ibn Khallikān, *Wafayāt al-aʿyān*, 4:212, 523–24; al-Dhahabī, *Taʾrīkh al-Islām*, 30:368–70; al-Yāfiʿī, *Mirʾāt al-jinān*, 3:75; al-Subkī, *Ṭabaqāt al-shāfiʿiyyah*, 3:62–63; al-Maqrīzī, *Ittiʿāẓ*, 2:267; Ibn al-ʿImād, *Shadharāt al-dhahab*, 3:293.

15 Including Muḥammad ibn Aḥmad al-Baghdādī ibn al-Qaṭṭān (d. 359/970), Aḥmad ibn ʿUmar al-Jīzī al-Zajjāj (fl. 4th/10th c.), and Muḥammad ibn Aḥmad al-Kāṭib (d. 399/1009).

16 Including Abū Naṣr ibn Mākūlā (d. 475/1082), Muḥammad ibn Abī Naṣr al-Ḥumaydī (d. ca. 450/1058), ʿAbd al-Jalīl al-Sāwī (fl. 5th/11th c.), Muḥammad ibn Barakāt (d. 520/1126), Sahl ibn Bishr al-Isfarāʾīnī (fl. 5th/11th c.), and Abū ʿAbd Allāh al-Rāzī (fl. 5th/11th c.).

17 Al-Dhahabī, *Taʾrīkh al-Islām*, 33:283, and *Siyar aʿlām al-nubalāʾ*, 19:124.

18 The catalog of a manuscript library in Kuwait attributes a fourteenth work titled *Iḥyāʾ al-ʿulūm* (*Revivifying the Branches of Knowledge*, Idārat al-Makhṭūṭāt wa-l-Maktabāt al-Islāmiyyah, catalog number 21561) to al-Quḍāʿī, an ascription that I have not yet been able to verify.

19 The earliest listing I have found of al-Quḍāʿī's books is Ibn ʿAsākir's *Taʾrīkh madīnat Dimashq*, 53:168–69, which lists the extant works *Light in the Heavens*, *The Transmissions*, *A Treasury of Virtues*, and *The Book of Reports*, and the lost works *The Merits of al-Shāfiʿī* and *Compendium of Teachers*.

20 Cited in a late source, Ismāʿīl Pāshā, *Hadiyyat al-ʿārifīn*, 6:70.

21 Yāqūt, *Irshād al-arīb*, 5:214; Ibn Khallikān, *Wafayāt al-aʿyān*, 4:523–24 and passim; al-Maqrīzī, *Khiṭaṭ*, 1:5 and passim (twenty-nine references in all), and *Ittiʿāẓ*, 2:267 (al-Maqrīzī mentions al-Quḍāʿī's *Khiṭaṭ* numerous times in his own *Khiṭaṭ*, but oddly does not do so in his biographical entry on al-Quḍāʿī in the *Muqaffā*, 5:710–11); al-Qalqashandī, *Ṣubḥ al-aʿshā*, 3:334, 339, and passim; Ibn Taghrī-Birdī, *Al-Nujūm al-zāhirah* 1:56, 4:47, and passim.

22 Al-Silafī, *Mashyakhat al-Rāzī*, 1:241–42; al-Maqrīzī, *Muqaffā*, 5:710; al-Qalqashandī, *Ṣubḥ al-aʿshā*, 3:279; al-Ziriklī, *Al-Aʿlām*, 7:16–17.

23 Ibn ʿAsākir, *Tārīkh madīnat Dimashq*, 53:168–69.

24 Ibid.

25 Ibn ʿAṭiyyah, *Fihrist*, 1:128; Ibn Bashkuwāl, *Kitāb al-Ṣilah*, 1:74.

26 Ibn Bashkuwāl, *Kitāb al-Ṣilah*, 1:132.

27 Ḥājjī Khalīfah, *Kashf al-ẓunūn*, 1:745.

28 Al-Silafī, *Mashyakhah*, 1:242.

29 Lane, "SH-H-B," *Lexicon*; it can also denote a firebrand, or a person who is sharp and penetrating.

30 In his French translation of *Kitāb al-Shihāb*, titled *Le Flambeau*, Khawam rearranges the collection thematically into the following chapters: (1) religion, (2) social relationships, (3) economic problems, (4) women, (5) respect for creation, (6) wealth and poverty, (7) daily life, (8) personal conduct, (9) the Qur'an, (10) politics, (11) the prophet speaking of himself, (12) the family, (13) supplications invoked by the prophet, and (14) words spoken by God and reported by God's messenger.

31 Cf. al-Silafī, *Mashyakhat al-Rāzī*, 1:241; Ibn ʿAṭiyyah, *Fihris*, 1:128; Ibn ʿAsākir, *Taʾrīkh madīnat Dimashq*, 53:169; Ibn Khallikān, *Wafayāt al-aʿyān*, 4:212, 523; al-Dhahabī, *Taʾrīkh al-Islām*, 30:369; al-Yāfiʿī, *Mirʾāt al-jinān*, 3:75; al-Subkī, *Ṭabaqāt al-Shāfiʿiyyah*, 3:62; al-Maqrīzī, *Muqaffā*, 5:710; al-ʿUkbarī, *Shadharāt al-dhahab*, 3:293.

32 Al-Silafī, *Mashyakhat al-Rāzī*, 1:242; Ibn ʿAsākir, *Taʾrīkh madīnat Dimashq*, 53:169. Also, Ibn Abī l-Rabīʿ al-Qaysī (fl. 6th/12th c.) from Granada wrote in verse, "The *Shihāb* has merit above other books, for it transcribes the words of the Arabian prophet; containing luminous sayings of wisdom and counsel of warning and promise and refinement" (al-Maqqarī, *Nafḥ al-ṭīb*, 2:138).

33 A full list of extant and lost works is available in Online Material > Book Supplements on the LAL website: www.libraryofarabicliterature.org.

34 Translated by a team of scholars in Ahmedabad and Vadodara; the English translation is by Zulqarnain Hakeemuddin.

35 Cf. Ibn al-Abbār, *Al-Takmilah li-Kitāb al-Ṣilah*, 1:67, 75, 213, 224, 263.

36 Al-Maqqarī, *Nafḥ al-ṭīb*, 5:342.

37 E.g., Ibn Bashkuwāl, *Kitāb al-Ṣilah*, 1:35, 74, 132.

38 Al-Rāfiʿī, *Al-Tadwīn* 2:468, 499, and passim.

39 Al-Dhahabī, *Taʾrīkh al-Islām*, 36:186.

40 Al-ʿAydarūsī, *Taʾrīkh al-nūr al-sāfir*, 1:47.

41 Al-Ṣāghānī, *Mashāriq al-anwār*, 35–36. He also composed a book titled *Al-Durr al-multaqaṭ* in which he listed fifty-six hadith (about 4 percent of the total hadiths in *Kitāb al-Shihāb*) that he claimed were weak or fabricated.

42 Al-Ṣāghānī, *Mashāriq al-anwār*, 35–36. Jonathan Brown has traced the process whereby al-Bukhārī and Muslim's compilations were gradually canonized, and al-Ṣāghānī's work

appears to have been part of that effort. See Brown, *The Canonization of al-Bukhārī and Muslim*, 367–77. Abū l-Faḍl al-ʿIrāqī (d. 806/1403) in *Risālah fī-l-radd ʿalā l-Ṣāghānī* refuted al-Ṣāghānī's assessment of the *Shihāb*, arguing for the soundness of the hadith that al-Ṣāghānī deemed weak.

43 Ibn al-Athīr, *Al-Mathal al-sāʾir*, 1:128.

44 Sayf al-Dīn, *Khazāʾin imām al-muttaqīn*, 76, 79–83; see also quotations from *Kitāb al-Shihāb* in his *Salsabīl ḥikam ghadaq*, 55–59.

45 The *Musnad al-Shihāb* manuscripts contain numerous study notices (*samāʿāt*) and certificates of transmission (*ijāzāt*); the *Kitāb al-Shihāb* and *Sharḥ al-Shihāb* manuscripts do not. This is presumably because scholars sought certification for transmitting hadith along with *isnād*s.

46 Along with another student named Abū Rūḥ Yāsīn ibn Sahl ibn al-Ḥasan al-Khashshāb al-Qāyinī; cf. study notice at end of *juzʾ* 3, fol. 164, and end of *juzʾ* 6, fol. 201.

47 The missing parts are *juzʾ* 2, the ending parts of *juzʾ* 4 and 5, and some folios in between (in this edition: §§1.154–2.19, 4.14–4.42, 4.90–4.100, and several individual hadiths from chs. 5–9). In *juzʾ* 5–17, the ordering of the hadiths is different from *Kitāb al-Shihāb*.

48 Note that *juzʾ* numbers are different in different manuscripts of *Musnad al-Shihāb*; most MSS are divided into ten *juzʾ*.

49 Cf. study notice on fols. 1, 23, 34, 38. The manuscript also contains a *samāʿ* notice dated 513/1119 on fol. 13.

50 The manuscript contains almost all of ch. 1 (§§1.88–1.154 and 1.161–1.169 are missing), and from ch. 2 it has §§2.1–2.43.

51 The catalog of the Ottoman Sultan Bayezid II's palace library compiled by his royal librarian in 907/1502 (MS Török F. 59 in the Hungarian National Library, fols. 27–28) lists five copies of *Kitāb al-Shihāb*. The Topkapi and Süleymaniye manuscripts I have used in the present edition could be two of these.

52 The full catalog number is listed (reading from right to left) as: ن س ١ ج ١ ن خ ٤٥٢ ن ع ٧٧٤. Cf. Sirāj al-Dīn and Zaydān, *Fihrist al-makhṭūṭāt*, 600–601.

53 Cf. fol. 3; also fol. 2, which has names of additional scholars who taught the text.

54 E.g., fols. 381, 325.

55 The missing folios are 180, 414, 417–20.

56 There are two further manuscripts from this period that I have not been able to obtain. The first is a manuscript of *Kitāb al-Shihāb* (or more likely, because of its length and title, a commentary on it) dated 596/1200 and located in the Maktabat Ruwāq al-Atrāk of al-Azhar Mosque (Jamiʿ al-Azhar) in Cairo, catalog number 791. It was used by al-Marāghī in his 1970 Cairo commentary titled *Al-Lubāb fī Sharḥ al-Shihāb*, in which he says (م)

that the manuscript contains 238 folios and is titled *Al-Qawl al-badīʿ*. The second is a manuscript of *Kitāb al-Shihāb* dated 718/1317 and located in the library of the American University in Beirut, catalog number MS039: M23e &Mic-MS-10 (*Kitāb al-Shihāb* is one of six titles copied together within a larger volume titled *Majmuʿah adabiyyah wa-dīniyyah*).

57 The *waqf* colophon on the title page names the Zaydī imam [Yaḥyā ibn Muḥammad] al-Mutawakkil ʿalā-llāh (r. 1904–48) as having ordered the manuscript to be placed in the General Waqf Library in 1343/1925. It was donated by a scholar named al-Mahdī ibn Aḥmad ibn al-Ḥasan.

58 The additional hadiths are

(١) المؤمن كالجمل الأنِف إن قِيد انقاد وإن أنيخ على صخرة استناخ.

(٢) إنّ هذا الإيمان يذهب الهمّ والحزن.

(٣) ثلاثة لا يمسّهم فتنة الدنيا والآخرة من نصح المسلمين ومن دلّ على الخير ومن رضي بقضاء الله وقدره.

(٤) ثلاثة لا يمسّهم النار يوم القيامة البارّ بوالديه والمرأة المطيعة لزوجها والعبد المؤدّي حقّ الله وحقّ مواليه.

(٥) ثلاثة يعصمهم الله من شرّ إبليس من أحبّ أصحابي ومن تمسّك بسنّتي ومن آمن بالقدر خيره وشرّه من الله عزّ وجلّ.

(٦) ثلاثة يستغفر لهم السموات السبع والأرضون السبع ومن فيهنّ من الملائكة المقرّبين والعلماء والمتعلّمون والعالمون.

(٧) ثلاثة تتلقّاهم الحور العين يوم القيامة الذاكرين الله والباكين من خشية الله والمستغفرين بالأسحار وفي أطراف النهار.

The first of these is added to §1.115 in the manuscripts of *Musnad al-Shihāb*, in the second report of the hadith.

59 The date of the manuscript is not mentioned, but the first and the final pages contain three study notices dated 601/1204, 602/1205, and 664/1265; the last reading is noted to have taken place in the Area of the Turks—Darb al-Atrāk—Cairo.

60 Among the scholars named on the first folio as teachers of this text is Abū Rajāʾ Hibat Allāh ibn Muḥammad ibn ʿAlī al-Shīrāzī. The title page contains a *waqf* notice for Madrasat al-Ḥāfiẓ Ḍiyāʾ al-Dīn al-Maqdisī in the area of Safḥ Qāsyūn near Damascus.

61 Catalog information can be found at http://yazmalar.gov.tr/detay_goster.php?k=32011#.

62 The first folio containing part of al-Quḍāʿī's introduction is missing, as is the last folio, and some inside folios.

63 Cf. fol. 51.

64 There are two notices of ownership on the first and last folios, the second dated 1170/1756. The manuscript contains no emendations or marginal additions.

65 Garrett, *Descriptive Catalog*, 4–5.

66 Al-Salafī used manuscripts [ظ] and [ت], as well as Ẓāhiriyyah 538 (listed in the present edition as MS 2 of the secondary manuscripts); see introduction to his edition, 15–18, MSS 1–3.

67 Al-Maḥallāwī used manuscript [م]; cf. introduction to his edition, 16–17, MS 1.

68 The transposed transcription “al-Siljimāsī” appears frequently for “al-Sijilmāsī” in Najmī’s edition (it is correctly transcribed as “al-Sijilmāsī” at 1:12, 20, 26).

69 It is unclear whether al-Quḍāʿī composed *Musnad al-Shihāb* first or *Kitāb al-Shihāb*, for the author’s introduction in each of the two refers the reader to the other. For this reason, it is difficult to gauge which of the additional hadiths are likely to be early copyist add-ons. Alternatively, al-Quḍāʿī himself could have included a few hadiths in one that he missed citing in the other.

70 Undated manuscripts of *Kitāb al-Shihāb* and relatively recent manuscripts from the 11th–13th/17th–19th centuries are found in abundance in manuscript libraries across the globe. For the purposes of this edition they are redundant, not offering anything new beyond what is already gleaned from the older manuscripts. But they afford a sense of the continuity and dissemination of the *Shihāb* manuscript tradition, and to this end, a sample list of six such manuscripts, and catalog information for several others, is provided on the LAL website.

71 For a handful of the sayings across the different manuscripts, there is some variation in sequence.

كتاب الشّهاب

Light in the Heavens

بسم الله الرحمن الرحيم

الحمد لله القادر الفرد الحكيم الفاطر الصمد الكريم باعث نبيّه محمّد صلّى الله عليه ١،٠
وآله وسلّم بجوامع الكَلِم وبدائع الحِكَم وجاعله للناس ﴿بَشِيرًا وَنَذِيرًا﴾ ﴿وَدَاعِيًا﴾ إليه ﴿بِإِذْنِهِ وَسِرَاجًا مُنِيرًا﴾ صلّى الله عليه وعلى آله الذين أذهب عنهم الرجس وطهّرهم تطهيرًا.

أمّا بعد فإنّ في الألفاظ النبويّة والآداب الشرعيّة جلاء لقلوب العارفين وشفاء ٢،٠
لأدواء الخائفين. لصدورها عن المؤيّد بالعصمة والمخصوص بالبيان والحكمة. الذي يدعو إلى الهدى ويبصّر من العمى ولا ﴿يَنطِقُ عَنِ ٱلْهَوَىٰٓ﴾. صلّى الله عليه أفضل ما صلّى على أحد من ﴿عِبَادِهِ ٱلَّذِينَ ٱصْطَفَىٰٓ﴾.

وقد جمعت في كتابي هذا ممّا سمعته من حديث رسول الله صلّى الله عليه وعلى ٣،٠
آله وسلّم ألف كلمة من الحكمة في الوصايا والآداب والمواعظ والأمثال. قد سلمت من التكلّف مبانيها وبعدت عن التعسّف معانيها وبانت بالتأييد عن فصاحة الفصحاء وتميّزت بهدي النبوّة عن بلاغة البلغاء. وجعلتها مسرودة يتلو بعضها بعضا محذوفة الأسانيد مبوّبة أبوابًا على حسب تقارب الألفاظ ليقرب تناولها ويسهل حفظها. وزدت مائتي كلمة فصارت ألف كلمة ومائتي كلمة. وختمت الكتاب بأدعية مرويّة عنه عليه السلام وأفردت لأسانيد جميعها كتابًا يُرجع في معرفتها إليه.

وأنا أسأل الله تعالى أن يجعل ما ٱعتمدته من ذلك خالصًا لوجهه ومقرّبًا من ٤،٠
رحمته بحوله وقوّته.

Author's Introduction

In the name of God, the merciful, the compassionate

God be praised! He is one, powerful and wise, the eternal and generous creator. He sent Muḥammad as a prophet, fortified with profound words and marvelous sayings, making him «a bringer of glad tidings and a warner»[1] for all people, «a caller» to him «with his permission, and a shining sun.»[2] May God bless him and also his progeny, from whom God stripped all forms of filth, and whom he made completely pure.[3] 0.1

The prophet's words and his divinely inspired directions for refined behavior burnish the hearts of those who know God and cure the diseases of those who fear him. For they come from one whom God has protected from error, who has been singled out to receive clear exposition and wisdom, who calls to right guidance, makes the blind see, and never «speaks from a whim.»[4] May God shower upon him the choicest blessings he has ever showered upon «his chosen servants.»[5] 0.2

In this book, I have collected one thousand wise sayings from the sayings of the messenger of God—including testaments, directions for refined behavior, counsels, and maxims—whose forms and meanings are free of artifice and discord. Inspired by God, they are superior to the expressive discourse of the masters of expression. Distinguished by the guidance of prophecy, they are loftier than the sayings of the masters of eloquence. I have arranged these sayings uninterruptedly, one following the other, omitting the chains of transmission. For simplified access and ease of memorization, I have divided them into chapters based on similarity of lexical pattern. I have subsequently added two hundred more sayings, to make twelve hundred in all.[6] I end the book with supplications attributed to the prophet. The chains of transmission for each hadith I have collected in a separate book; they can be examined there.[7] 0.3

I ask God—through his might and power—to let my efforts be directed to winning his acceptance, and to seeking his merciful gaze. 0.4

الباب الأوّل

الأعمال بالنيّات ١٠١

المجالس بالأمانة ٢،١

المستشار مؤتمن ٣،١

العِدة عطيّة ٤،١

العِدة دَين ٥،١

الحرب خُدعة ٦،١

الندم توبة ٧،١

الجماعة رحمة والفُرقة عذاب ٨،١

الأمانة غنى ٩،١

الدين النصيحة ١٠،١

الحسب المال والكرم التقوى ١١،١

الخير عادة والشرّ لَجاجة ١٢،١

السماح رَباح والعسر شؤم ١٣،١

Chapter One

Acts are only worth the intentions that accompany them. 1.1

Keep what is said at gatherings private. 1.2

Advice is sought in trust. 1.3

A promise to give is binding. 1.4

A promise is a debt. 1.5

Warfare entails cunning. 1.6

Regret is a form of repentance. 1.7

Unity is mercy, dissent punishment. 1.8

Integrity is a form of wealth. 1.9

True faith is giving good counsel. 1.10

Virtue is wealth,[8] magnanimity piety. 1.11

Goodness is habitual, wickedness obstinacy. 1.12

Leniency brings dividends, harshness deficits. 1.13

الحزم سوء الظنّ ١٤،١

الولد مَبْخَلة مَجبنة ١٥،١

البَذاء من الجفاء ١٦،١

القرآن هو الدواء ١٧،١

الدعاء هو العبادة ١٨،١

الدَّين شين الدِّين ١٩،١

التدبير نصف العيش ٢٠،١

التودّد نصف العقل ٢١،١

الهمّ نصف الهرم ٢٢،١

وقلّة العيال أحد اليسارَين ٢٣،١

حسن السؤال نصف العلم ٢٤،١

السلام قبل الكلام ٢٥،١

الرضاع يغيّر الطباع ٢٦،١

البركة مع أكابركم ٢٧،١

مِلاك العمل خواتمه ٢٨،١

كرم الكتاب ختمه ٢٩،١

Prudence is to expect the worst. 1.14

Offspring cause stinginess and timidity. 1.15

Obscenities offend. 1.16

The Qur'an is the real cure. 1.17

Supplication is the best form of worship. 1.18

Debt disfigures devotion. 1.19

Half of living well is planning well. 1.20

Half of discernment is affection. 1.21

Worry causes aging.[9] 1.22

The fewer children you have, the more affluent you will be.[10] 1.23

Half of learning is asking good questions. 1.24

Greet before conversing. 1.25

One's nature is influenced by the milk one has suckled.[11] 1.26

Elders bring blessings. 1.27

The outcome is the essence of a deed. 1.28

Honor the book by reading it in full.[12] 1.29

ملاك الدين الورع ١،٣٠

خشية الله رأس كلّ حكمة والورع سيّد العمل ١،٣١

مَطل الغنيّ ظلم ومسألة الغنيّ نار ١،٣٢

التحدّث بالنعم شكر ١،٣٣

انتظار الفرج بالصبر عبادة ١،٣٤

الصوم[١] جُنّة ١،٣٥

الزعيم غارم ١،٣٦

الرفق رأس الحكمة ١،٣٧

كلمة الحكمة ضالّة كلّ حكيم ١،٣٨

البرّ[٢] حسن الخلق ١،٣٩

الشباب شعبة من الجنون ١،٤٠

النساء حبائل الشيطان ١،٤١

الخمر جماع الإثم ١،٤٢

الخمر أمّ الخبائث ١،٤٣

الغُلول من جمر جهنّم ١،٤٤

---

١ ظ، م: رواية إضافيّة (الصيام). ٢ م: (اليمن).

Faith is bolstered by scrupulosity. 1.30

The pinnacle of wisdom is fear of God, and the prince of deeds scrupulosity. 1.31

The wealthy oppress when they delay payment and court hellfire when they beg. 1.32

To speak of favors received is to show gratitude. 1.33

Awaiting succor with fortitude is the best form of worship. 1.34

Fasting gives protection. 1.35

A chieftain is a guarantor for his tribe. 1.36

Gentleness is the pinnacle of wisdom. 1.37

The sage should seek out wise words wherever they may roam.[13] 1.38

Goodness is beauty of character. 1.39

Youth is a time of madness. 1.40

Women are Satan's snares. 1.41

All sins converge in wine. 1.42

Wine is the mother of all abominations. 1.43

Embezzlement burns with a fire from hell. 1.44

النياحة من عمل الجاهليّة ٤٥،١

الزنا يورث الفقر ٤٦،١

زنا العيون النظر ٤٧،١

الحُمّى رائد الموت ٤٨،١

الحُمّى من فَيح جهنّم ٤٩،١

الحُمّى حظّ كلّ مؤمن من النار ٥٠،١

القناعة مال لا ينفد ٥١،١

الأمانة تجرّ الرزق والخيانة تجرّ الفقر ٥٢،١

الصُّبْحة تمنع الرزق ٥٣،١

العمائم تيجان العرب ٥٤،١

الحياء خيرٌ كلّه ٥٥،١

الحياء لا يأتي إلّا بخير ٥٦،١

المسجد بيت كلّ تقيّ ٥٧،١

آفة العلم النسيان ٥٨،١

وآفة الحديث الكذب ٥٩،١

وآفة الحلم السفه ٦٠،١

وآفة العبادة الفترة ٦١،١

Wailing for the dead is a practice from the dark ages.[14] 1.45

Fornication bequeaths poverty. 1.46

To ogle is to fornicate with the eyes. 1.47

Fever is a scout sent by death. 1.48

Fever is a blaze from the inferno. 1.49

Fever is the believer's share of hellfire.[15] 1.50

Contentment is wealth that is never used up. 1.51

Integrity brings sustenance, fraud brings poverty. 1.52

Late risers earn no pay. 1.53

An Arab's turban is his crown. 1.54

All good things converge in modesty. 1.55

Modesty brings nothing but good. 1.56

The mosque is where the pious live. 1.57

Forgetfulness is the bane of learning. 1.58

Falsehood is the bane of conversation. 1.59

Foolhardiness is the bane of prudence. 1.60

Indolence is the bane of worship. 1.61

وآفة الشجاعة البغي ٦٢،١

وآفة السماحة المنّ ٦٣،١

وآفة الجمال الخُيَلاء ٦٤،١

وآفة الجود السَّرَف ٦٥،١

وآفة الحسب الفخر ٦٦،١

وآفة الظرف الصَّلَف ٦٧،١

وآفة الدين الهوى ٦٨،١

السعيد من وُعظ بغيره والشقيّ من شَقي في بطن أمّه ٦٩،١

كفّارة الذنب الندامة ٧٠،١

الجمعة حجّ المساكين[١] ٧١،١

الحجّ جهاد كلّ ضعيف ٧٢،١

وجهاد المرأة حسن التبعُّل ٧٣،١

طلب الحلال جهاد ٧٤،١

موت الغريب شهادة ٧٥،١

---

١ م: تضيف نسخة في الهامش (الفقراء).

Injustice is the bane of bravery. 1.62

Keeping tally is the bane of generosity. 1.63

Conceit is the bane of beauty. 1.64

Waste is the bane of liberality. 1.65

Arrogance is the bane of a good pedigree. 1.66

Bragging is the bane of refinement. 1.67

Caprice is the bane of faith. 1.68

The fortunate are those who have learned from others, the wretched have been wretched since the womb. 1.69

Repentance makes for atonement. 1.70

The Friday prayer is the hajj of the poor. 1.71

Hajj is the jihad of the frail. 1.72

Being a good wife is a woman's jihad. 1.73

Making an honest living is a form of jihad. 1.74

Dying in a foreign land is a form of martyrdom. 1.75

العلم لا يحلّ منعه ١،٧٦

الشاهد يرى ما لا يرى الغائب ١،٧٧

الدالّ على الخير كفاعله ١،٧٨

ساقي القوم آخرهم شربًا ١،٧٩

كلّ معروف صدقة ١،٨٠

مُداراة الناس صدقة ١،٨١

الكلمة الطيّبة صدقة ١،٨٢

ما وقى به المرء عرضه كتب له به صدقة ١،٨٣

الصدقة على القرابة صدقة وصِلة ١،٨٤

الصدقة تمنع ميتة السوء ١،٨٥

وصدقة السرّ تطفئ غضب الربّ ١،٨٦

صلة الرحم تزيد في العمر ١،٨٧

فعل المعروف يقي مصارع السوء[١] ١،٨٨

الرجل في ظلّ صدقته حتى يقضي بين الناس ١،٨٩

الصدقة تطفئ الخطيئة كما يطفئ الماء النار ١،٩٠

المعتدي في الصدقة كمانعها ١،٩١

---

١ م: رواية إضافيّة (صنائع المعروف تقي مصارع السوء).

Knowledge must not be withheld. 1.76

Those present see what the absent do not. 1.77

Those who prompt others to do good are rewarded in like measure. 1.78

The water carrier is the last to drink. 1.79

Charity is any generous act. 1.80

Charity is kindness to others. 1.81

Charity is a kind word. 1.82

Protecting one's honor counts as charity. 1.83

Charity to family counts twice: as charity and as nurture. 1.84

Charity protects against a bad death. 1.85

Charity in secret assuages the lord's wrath. 1.86

Nurturing relatives brings long life. 1.87

Generosity protects against a horrible death. 1.88

A man can enjoy the shade of his charity till he sits in judgment. 1.89

Charity extinguishes sin as water extinguishes fire. 1.90

Charity to the undeserving is like refusing to give at all.[16] 1.91

التائب من الذنب كمن لا ذنب له ٩٢،١

الظلم ظلمات يوم القيامة ٩٣،١

كثرة الضحك تميت القلب ٩٤،١

في كلّ كبد حرّى[١] أجر ٩٥،١

العلماء أمناء الله على خلقه ٩٦،١

رأس الحكمة مخافة الله ٩٧،١

الجنّة دار الأسخياء ٩٨،١

الجنّة تحت ظلال السيوف ٩٩،١

الجنّة تحت أقدام الأمّهات ١٠٠،١

الدعاء بين الأذان والإقامة لا يُرَدّ ١٠١،١

كسب[٢] الحلال فريضة بعد الفريضة ١٠٢،١

أعظم النساء بركة أقلّهنّ مؤونة ١٠٣،١

المؤمن مرآة المؤمن ١٠٤،١

المؤمن أخو المؤمن ١٠٥،١

١ ك، م، ت: رواية إضافيّة (رطبة). ٢ ك، ت، م: رواية إضافيّة (طلب).

Penitence is as good as not sinning. 1.92

Judgment day will be ominously dark for the tyrant.[17] 1.93

Too much hilarity kills the spirit. 1.94

Compassionate hearts will be rewarded.[18] 1.95

God charges the learned to look after his creatures. 1.96

The pinnacle of wisdom is fear of God. 1.97

Paradise will be home to the generous. 1.98

Paradise is shaded by righteous swords.[19] 1.99

Paradise lies beneath your mother's feet. 1.100

Supplications made between the call and summons to prayer are never rebuffed.[20] 1.101

An honest living is an obligation second only to worship. 1.102

A good woman makes few demands. 1.103

Believers are mirrors for each other. 1.104

Believers are brothers to each other. 1.105

Believers do not ask for much. 1.106

Believers are intelligent, astute, and cautious. 1.107

Believers are friendly and approachable. 1.108

Believers can be trusted with life and property. 1.109

Believers are generous and guileless, libertines are depraved and shameless. 1.110

Believers buttress and support each other. 1.111

The true believer among the faithful is like the head to the body. 1.112

Believers will be shaded by their charity on judgment day. 1.113

One mouthful is enough for the believer; the unbeliever craves seven.[21] 1.114

Believers are gentle and easygoing. 1.115

Winter is springtime for the believer.[22] 1.116

Supplication is the believer's best weapon. 1.117

Ritual-prayer illumines the believer. 1.118

The world is prison for the believer, paradise for the unbeliever. 1.119

The sage should seek out wisdom wherever it may roam.[23] 1.120

A believer's intentions reach farther than his deeds. 1.121

A supplicant at the door is a gift from God to believers. 1.122

Death is a gift for believers. 1.123

شرف المؤمن قيامه بالليل وعزّه ٱستغناؤه عن الناس ١٢٤،١

العلم خليل المؤمن والحلم وزيره والعقل دليله والعمل قائده والرفق والده والبرّ أخوه ١٢٥،١
والصبر أمير جنوده

الغيرة من الإيمان ١٢٦،١

الحياء من الإيمان ١٢٧،١

البذاذة من الإيمان ١٢٨،١

الصبر نصف الإيمان واليقين الإيمان كلّه ١٢٩،١

الإيمان نصفان نصف شكر ونصف صبر ١٣٠،١

الإيمان يمانٍ والحكمة يمانيّة ١٣١،١

الإيمان قيّد الفتك ١٣٢،١

عَلَمَ الإيمان الصلاة ١٣٣،١

المسلم من سلم المسلمون من لسانه ويده ١٣٤،١

المسلم أخو المسلم لا يظلمه ولا يُسلمه ١٣٥،١

المسلمون يد واحدة على من سواهم ١٣٦،١

الموت كفّارة لكلّ مسلم ١٣٧،١

طلب العلم فريضة على كلّ مسلم ١٣٨،١

Nights of prayer bestow honor on a believer, self-sufficiency gives him glory. 1.124

Knowledge is the friend of the believer, maturity his advisor, intelligence his guide, deeds his shepherd, gentleness his father, kindness his brother, and patience the commander of his armies. 1.125

Faith includes a jealous sense of honor. 1.126

Faith includes modesty. 1.127

Faith includes wearing old clothes. 1.128

Forbearance is half of faith, conviction the whole. 1.129

Faith has two halves: gratitude and forbearance. 1.130

Faith and wisdom hail from Yemen.[24] 1.131

Faith shackles aggression. 1.132

The ritual-prayer is the banner of faith. 1.133

A Muslim is someone whose tongue and hand no other Muslim fears. 1.134

A Muslim is brother to a Muslim—he neither oppresses him nor hands him over. 1.135

Muslims are a united front, like one hand. 1.136

Death is sufficient atonement for Muslims. 1.137

It is the duty of all Muslims to seek knowledge.[25] 1.138

كلّ المسلم على المسلم حرام دمه وعِرضه وماله ١٣٩،١

حرمة مال المسلم كحرمة دمه ١٤٠،١

المهاجر من هجر ما حرّم الله عليه[1] ١٤١،١

المجاهد من جاهد نفسه في طاعة الله ١٤٢،١

الكيّس من دان نفسه وعمل لما بعد الموت والعاجز من أتبع نفسه هواها وتمنّى على الله ١٤٣،١

المرء كثير بأخيه ١٤٤،١

المرء على دين خليله ١٤٥،١

المرء مع من أحبّ ١٤٦،١

كرم المرء دينه ومروءته عقله وحسَبه خلقه ١٤٧،١

من حسن إسلام المرء تركه ما لا يعنيه ١٤٨،١

الناس كأسنان المُشط ١٤٩،١

الناس معادن كمعادن الذهب والفضّة ١٥٠،١

الناس كإبل مائة لا تجد فيها راحلة واحدة ١٥١،١

---

١ ظ، ت، م: رواية إضافيّة (ما نهى الله عنه)، وفي هامش ك: (ما نهاه الله عنه).

Blood, honor, and property are sacrosanct for every Muslim. 1.139

A Muslim's property is as inviolable as his life. 1.140

The true emigrant is one who rejects God's prohibitions.[26] 1.141

A true warrior battles his urges in order to obey God. 1.142

The intelligent man curbs his urges and prepares for the afterlife. The incompetent man follows every whim and urge yet still expects God to fulfill his wishes. 1.143

Aided by his brother, one man is like many. 1.144

A man is swayed by what his friend believes. 1.145

A man keeps company with those he loves.[27] 1.146

A man's religion is his real honor, intelligence his real virility, and character his real breeding. 1.147

Commitment to God is commendable only when you avoid what does not concern you.[28] 1.148

People are like the teeth of a comb. 1.149

People are like quarries of gold and silver.[29] 1.150

People are like a herd of a hundred camels—it is hard to single one out.[30] 1.151

الغنى اليأس ممّا في أيدي الناس ١٥٢،١

رأس العقل بعد الإيمان[١] التودّد إلى الناس ١٥٣،١

كلّ ٱمرئ حسيب نفسه ١٥٤،١

كلّ ما هوآت قريب ١٥٥،١

كلّ عين زانية ١٥٦،١

كلّ شيء بقدَر حتى العجز والكيس ١٥٧،١

كلّ صاحب علم غَرثان إلى علم ١٥٨،١

ولكلّ شيء عماد وعماد هذا الدين الفقه ١٥٩،١

كلّ مشكل حرام وليس في الدين إشكال ١٦٠،١

كلّكم راع وكلّكم مسؤول عن رعيّته ١٦١،١

لكلّ غادر لواء يوم القيامة بقدر غدرته ١٦٢،١

أوّل ما يُقضى بين الناس يوم القيامة في الدماء ١٦٣،١

أوّل ما يحاسَب به الصلاة ١٦٤،١

أوّل ما يوضع في الميزان الخلق الحسن ١٦٥،١

أوّل ما يُرفع من هذه الأمّة الحياء والأمانة ١٦٦،١

---

١ ك: تضيف في الهامش مع علامة التصحيح (بالله).

True wealth means not coveting another's property. 1.152

After faith, affability is the pinnacle of intelligence. 1.153

Every man is his own assessor.[31] 1.154

All that will be is at hand. 1.155

Every eye fornicates. 1.156

Everything, even incapacity and aptitude, depends on fate. 1.157

The man of learning thirsts for knowledge. 1.158

Everything has a foundation—discernment is the foundation of our religion. 1.159

Every dubious thing is forbidden—nothing dubious can be part of religion. 1.160

Each and every one of you is a shepherd accountable for his flock. 1.161

On judgment day, all deceivers shall have the extent of their deception 1.162
advertised.

On judgment day, cases of bloodshed will be judged first. 1.163

The ritual-prayer will be assessed first. 1.164

Good character will be placed in the celestial scale first. 1.165

Modesty and trustworthiness will be the first things to disappear from our 1.166
community.

أوّل ما تفقدون من دينكم الأمانة وآخر ما تفقدون الصلاة ١٦٧،١

الودّ يُتوارث والبغض يتوارث ١٦٨،١

حبّك الشيء يُعمي ويُصِمّ ١٦٩،١

الهديّة تذهب بالسمع والبصر ١٧٠،١

الخير معقود بنواصي[1] الخيل إلى يوم القيامة ١٧١،١

يمن الخيل في شُقرها ١٧٢،١

السفر قطعة من العذاب ١٧٣،١

طاعة النساء ندامة ١٧٤،١

البلاء موكّل بالمنطق[2] ١٧٥،١

الصيام نصف الصبر وعلى كلّ شيء زكاة وزكاة الجسد الصيام ١٧٦،١

الصائم لا تردّ دعوته ١٧٧،١

الصوم في الشتاء الغنيمة الباردة ١٧٨،١

السواك يزيد الرجل فصاحة ١٧٩،١

جمال الرجل فصاحة لسانه ١٨٠،١

---

١ ا، ت، م: رواية إضافيّة (في نواصي). ٢ ا: رواية إضافيّة (بالقول).

Trustworthiness will be the first part of faith to be lost, ritual-prayer the last. 1.167

Love and hate are both hereditary. 1.168

Love of a thing makes you deaf and blind. 1.169

Gifts affect what you see and hear. 1.170

Goodness will be braided into your horses' forelocks until judgment day.[32] 1.171

Chestnut horses bring good luck. 1.172

Travel is a foretaste of the punishment. 1.173

Obeying women causes regret. 1.174

Words court disaster. 1.175

Fasting is one half of forbearance. There is levy on all things—the body's is fasting. 1.176

The supplication of a fasting person is never rebuffed. 1.177

Fasting in winter is easy pickings. 1.178

Clean teeth enhance a man's eloquence. 1.179

Eloquent speech makes a man beautiful. 1.180

الإمام ضامن والمؤذّن مؤتمَن ١٨١،١

المؤذّنون أطول الناس أعناقًا يوم القيامة ١٨٢،١

شفاعتي لأهل الكبائر من أمّتي ١٨٣،١

الأنصار كرشي وعيبتي ١٨٤،١

يد الله على الجماعة ١٨٥،١

الصمت حُكم وقليل فاعله ١٨٦،١

الرزق أشدّ طلبًا للعبد من أجله ١٨٧،١

الرفق في المعيشة خير من بعض التجارة ١٨٨،١

التاجر الجبان محروم والتاجر الجسور مرزوق ١٨٩،١

حسن المَلَكَة نماء وسوء الملكة شؤم ١٩٠،١

فضوح الدنيا أهون من فضوح الآخرة ١٩١،١

القبر أوّل منزل من منازل الآخرة ١٩٢،١

الصبر عند الصدمة الأولى ١٩٣،١

دفن البنات من المكرمات ١٩٤،١

معترك المنايا ما بين الستّين إلى السبعين ١٩٥،١

The muezzin is given a task to perform, the prayer-leader has trust placed in him.[33] 1.181

On judgment day, muezzins will stand tall.[34] 1.182

I will intercede for my community's gravest sinners. 1.183

The Allies are my companions and confidants.[35] 1.184

God's hand protects the congregation. 1.185

Silence shows wisdom, but few oblige. 1.186

God's sustenance finds his servants more unerringly than death. 1.187

Living thriftily is more profitable than certain trades. 1.188

Timid traders fail, bold traders succeed. 1.189

Kind employers profit, mean employers lose. 1.190

This world's calamities are lighter than the hereafter's. 1.191

The grave is the first stopping place in your journey to the hereafter. 1.192

Fortitude is tested by the first shock. 1.193

Laying daughters to rest is an honorable deed.[36] 1.194

Death strikes between sixty and seventy years of age. 1.195

أعمار أمّتي ما بين السـتّين إلى السبعين ١٩٦،١

المكر والخديعة في النار ١٩٧،١

اليمين على نيّة المستحلف ١٩٨،١

الحلف حنث أو ندم ١٩٩،١

اليمين الفاجرة تدع الديار بلاقع ٢٠٠،١

اليمين الكاذبة منفقة للسلعة ممحقة للكسب ٢٠١،١

السلام تحيّة لملّتنا وأمان لذمّتنا ٢٠٢،١

علم لا ينفع ككنز لا يُنفَق منه ٢٠٣،١

الطاعم الشاكر له مثل أجر الصائم الصابر ٢٠٤،١

الصلاة قربان كلّ تقيّ ٢٠٥،١

بين العبد وبين الكفر ترك الصلاة ٢٠٦،١

موضع الصلاة من الدين كموضع الرأس من الجسد ٢٠٧،١

صلاة القاعد على النصف من صلاة القائم ٢٠٨،١

الزكاة قنطرة الإسلام ٢٠٩،١

Members of my community live until they are between sixty and seventy.[37] 1.196

Deception and duplicity guarantee hellfire. 1.197

Oaths are construed according to the requester.[38] 1.198

An egregious oath spawns sin or remorse. 1.199

Fraudulent oaths devastate the land. 1.200

False oaths deplete possessions and destroy livelihood. 1.201

The greeting of our people is "Peace," our subjects' security.[39] 1.202

Knowledge that brings no benefit is like hoarded treasure. 1.203

Gratitude after eating is like forbearance during fasting. 1.204

The pious draw near to God through ritual-prayer. 1.205

All that separates a man from unbelief is neglect of the ritual-prayer. 1.206

Prayer is to religion as the head to the body. 1.207

Ritual-prayer performed while sitting is worth half of one performed while standing. 1.208

The alms-levy is the trestle of Islam. 1.209

طيب الرجل ما ظهر ريحه وخفي لونه وطيب النساء ما ظهر لونه وخفي ريحه ٢١٠،١

التراب ربيع الصبيان ٢١١،١

الأرواح جنود مجنّدة فما تعارف منها ٱئتلف وما تناكر منها ٱختلف ٢١٢،١

الصدق طمأنينة والكذب ريبة ٢١٣،١

القرآن غنى لا فقر بعده ولا غنى دونه ٢١٤،١

الإيمان بالقدر يُذهب الهمّ والحزن ٢١٥،١

الزهد في الدنيا يريح القلب والبدن والرغبة في الدنيا تُكثر الهمّ والحزن والبطالة تُقسي القلب ٢١٦،١

العالم والمتعلّم شريكان في الخير ٢١٧،١

على اليد ما أخذت حتّى تؤدّيه ٢١٨،١

الولد للفراش وللعاهر الحجر ٢١٩،١

الضيافة على أهل الوَبَر وليست على أهل المدر ٢٢٠،١

للسائل حقّ وإن جاء على فرس ٢٢١،١

أيّ داء أدوأ[١] من البخل ٢٢٢،١

العائد في هبته كالكلب يعود في قَيئه ٢٢٣،١

١ م: رواية إضافيّة (أدوى).

A man's perfume is intense in fragrance and discreet in color. A woman's perfume is discreet in fragrance and intense in color. 1.210

Playing in dirt is a child's delight.[40] 1.211

Souls are like mustered armies: the similar come together and unite, the dissimilar part ways. 1.212

Truth comforts, falsehood disquiets. 1.213

The Qur'an is true wealth: no poverty with it, no wealth without. 1.214

Belief in destiny dispels troubles and grief. 1.215

Renouncing the world brings solace to heart and body, preoccupation with the world increases troubles and grief, and idleness hardens the heart. 1.216

Teacher and student are partners in the good. 1.217

Hands are burdened until they return what they have taken.[41] 1.218

Married couples can claim their offspring, adulterers can claim only their punishment—stones.[42] 1.219

Tent dwellers must provide hospitality, house dwellers need not.[43] 1.220

Every suppliant is deserving, even if he comes on a horse.[44] 1.221

Is there a disease worse than stinginess? 1.222

Taking back your gifts is like dogs licking their vomit. 1.223

النظر إلى الخضرة يزيد في البصر والنظر إلى المرأة الحسناء يزيد في البصر ٢٢٤،١

أمّتي الغرّ المحجّلون يوم القيامة من آثار الوضوء ٢٢٥،١

التصفيح للنساء والتسبيح للرجال ٢٢٦،١

النظرة سهم مسموم من سهام إبليس ٢٢٧،١

الشؤم في المرأة والفرس والدار ٢٢٨،١

نعمتان مغبون فيهما كثير من الناس الصحّة والفراغ ٢٢٩،١

ويل للعرب من شرّ قد ٱقترب ٢٣٠،١

الجبن والجرأة غرائز يضعها الله حيث يشاء ٢٣١،١

من كنز البرّ كتمان المصائب والأمراض والصدقة ٢٣٢،١

من سعادة المرأ أن يشبه أباه ٢٣٣،١

من سعادة المرأ حسن الخلق ٢٣٤،١

أهل المعروف في الدنيا هم أهل المعروف في الآخرة ٢٣٥،١

الخازن الأمين الذي يعطي ما أُمر به طيّبة به نفسه أحد المتصدّقَين ٢٣٦،١

السلطان ظلّ الله في الأرض يأوي إليه كلّ مظلوم ٢٣٧،١

Looking at greenery improves your eyesight, as does looking at a beautiful woman.[45] 1.224

On judgment day, my community's faces will glow and their limbs will gleam from their ablutions. 1.225

Women should clap, men should say "God be praised!"[46] 1.226

The gaze is one of Satan's poisoned arrows. 1.227

Women, horses, and homes can be ill-omened. 1.228

Most people take two blessings for granted—health and leisure. 1.229

Woe to the Arabs from an evil that has drawn near! 1.230

God apportions at will the traits of cowardice and boldness. 1.231

Piety's treasures include concealing three things: suffering, illness, and almsgiving. 1.232

A man is fortunate to resemble his father. 1.233

A man is fortunate to have a beautiful character. 1.234

Be generous in this world and be treated generously in the hereafter. 1.235

A trustworthy custodian, who willingly hands over what he is ordered to, earns the reward of the almsgiver. 1.236

The ruler is God's shadow on earth, a refuge for the wronged. 1.237

كلام ٱبن آدم كلّه عليه لا له إلّا أمرًا بمعروف أو نهيًا عن منكر أو ذكرًا لله تعالى ١٫٢٣٨

التُّؤَدة[1] والإقتصاد والصمت والتثبّت جزء من ستّة وعشرين جزءًا من النبوّة ١٫٢٣٩

الأنبياء قادة والفقهاء سادة ومجالستهم زيادة ١٫٢٤٠

المتشبّع بما لا يملك[2] كَلابس ثوبَي زور ١٫٢٤١

الوضوء قبل الطعام ينفي الفقر وبعده ينفي اللمم ويُصحّ البصر ١٫٢٤٢

القاصّ ينتظر المقت والمستمع إليه ينتظر الرحمة ١٫٢٤٣

والتاجر ينتظر الرزق والمحتكر ينتظر اللعنة ١٫٢٤٤

السعادة كلّ السعادة طول العمر في طاعة الله ١٫٢٤٥

الشقيّ كلّ الشقيّ من أدركته الساعة حيًّا لم يمت ١٫٢٤٦

الويل كلّ الويل لمن ترك عياله بخير وقدم على ربّه بشرّ ١٫٢٤٧

دعوة المظلوم مستجابة وإن كان فاجرًا ففجوره على نفسه ١٫٢٤٨

ثلاث دعوات مستجابات لا شكّ فيهنّ دعوة المظلوم ودعوة المسافر ودعوة الوالد على ولده ١٫٢٤٩

---

١ م: (التودّد). ٢ ك: (لم يُعطَه).

The only words uttered by Adam's children that count in their favor and not against them are commanding good, forbidding evil, and praising God. 1.238

Deliberation, moderation, steadfastness, and silence—these together make up one fraction of prophethood.[47] 1.239

Prophets are leaders, and scholars are masters—keeping their company brings benefits. 1.240

Boasting about something you do not have is like wearing two false garments.[48] 1.241

Washing your hands before eating dispels poverty; washing them after dispels dementia and keeps your eyes sharp. 1.242

Tellers of tales can expect malice; their audience can expect mercy.[49] 1.243

Traders can expect sustenance; hoarders can expect damnation. 1.244

A long life in obedience to God is the greatest good fortune. 1.245

The greatest wretch is the one alive, not dead, at the last hour. 1.246

Those who provide for their families after death, but appear before their lord with only sins to account for, will wail the loudest. 1.247

The supplications of the wronged will be answered, but they will be accountable for their own sins. 1.248

Three kinds of supplications are never denied: a victim's, a traveler's, and a father's against his son. 1.249

القضاة ثلاثة قاضيان في النار وقاض في الجنّة ١،٢٥٠

خصلتان لا تكونان في منافق حسن سمت ولا فقه في الدين ١،٢٥١

خصلتان لا تجتمعان في مؤمن البخل وسوء الخلق ١،٢٥٢

عينان لا تمسّهما النار يوم القيامة[1] عين بكت في جوف الليل من خشية الله وعين ١،٢٥٣
باتت تحرس في سبيل الله

منهومان لا يشبعان طالب علم وطالب دنيا ١،٢٥٤

الشيخ شابّ في حبّ ٱثنين في حبّ طول الحياة وكثرة المال ١،٢٥٥

أربعة يبغضهم الله تعالى البيّاع الحلّاف والفقير المختال والشيخ الزاني والإمام الجائر ١،٢٥٦

ثلاث مهلكات وثلاث منجيات فالثلاث المهلكات شحّ مطاع وهوى متّبع وإعجاب ١،٢٥٧
المرء بنفسه والثلاث المنجيات خشية الله في السرّ والعلانية والقصد في الفقر والغنى
والعدل في الغضب والرضى

المستبّان ما قالا فهو على البادي منهما حتّى يعتدي المظلوم ١،٢٥٨

أنا فَرَطكم على الحوض ١،٢٥٩

أنا وكافل اليتيم كهاتين في الجنّة وأشار بالسبّابة والوسطى ١،٢٦٠

أنا النذير والموت المغير والساعة الموعد ١،٢٦١

---

١ ا، م: حذفت (يوم القيامة).

Of every three judges, two are in hellfire, one in paradise.[50] 1.250

Two traits are never encountered in a hypocrite: virtuous conduct and knowl- 1.251
edge of religious practice.

Two traits never come together in a believer: parsimony and dissoluteness. 1.252

Two pairs of eyes will not be scorched on judgment day: eyes that shed tears in 1.253
the dark of night from fear of God, and eyes that stay awake to guard God's path.

Two kinds of people never have enough: seekers of knowledge and seekers of 1.254
worldly gain.

Old men resemble the young in their love of two things: long life and great wealth. 1.255

God hates four kinds of people: oath-swearing traders, arrogant beggars, dirty 1.256
old lechers, and tyrannical rulers.

Three traits damn, three save. Giving in to greed, following whims, and being 1.257
full of oneself damn. Fearing God in private and public, moderation in poverty and wealth, and dispensing justice in anger and calm save.

In a mutual curse, the instigator remains at fault unless the victim goes too far. 1.258

I will be the first of you to drink at the celestial pool. 1.259

The person who cares for the orphan and I will be as close as this in paradise— 1.260
he held up his index and middle finger.

I am the warner, death is the reaper, and the hour is determined. 1.261

الباب الثاني

من صمت نجا ١،٢

من تواضع لله رفعه الله ومن تكبّر وضعه الله ٢،٢

من يتألّ على الله يُكذبه ٣،٢

ومن يغفر يغفر الله له ٤،٢

ومن يعف يعف الله عنه ٥،٢

ومن يصبر على الرزيّة يعوّضه الله ٦،٢

ومن يكظم يأجره الله ٧،٢

ومن قدّر رزقه الله ومن بذّر حرمه الله ٨،٢

من نوقش الحساب عُذّب ٩،٢

من بدا جفا ١٠،٢

ومن ٱتّبع الصيد غفل ١١،٢

ومن ٱقترب من أبواب السلطان ٱفتتَن ١٢،٢

Chapter Two

Those who keep silent are saved. 2.1

God exalts those who are humble before him, and humbles those who are arrogant. 2.2

God proves wrong those who swear they know his judgments. 2.3

God forgives those who forgive others. 2.4

God pardons those who pardon others. 2.5

God rewards those who bear hardship with fortitude. 2.6

God recompenses those who curb their anger. 2.7

God sustains those who are restrained and denies those who are wasteful. 2.8

Those who are called up for interrogation at judgment will be punished. 2.9

Those who take to the desert become hardened. 2.10

Those who hunt to distraction become heedless. 2.11

Those who linger at a ruler's gates are tempted. 2.12

من قُتل دون ماله فهو شهيد ١٣،٢

من قتل دون أهله فهو شهيد ١٤،٢

من قتل دون دينه فهو شهيد[١] ١٥،٢

من يرد الله به خيرًا يصب منه ١٦،٢

من يرد الله به خيرًا يفقّهه في الدين ١٧،٢

من يرد الله به خيرًا يجعل خلقه حسناً[٢] ١٨،٢

من ٱشتاق إلى الجنة سارع إلى الخيرات ١٩،٢

ومن أشفق عن النار لَهَا عن الشهوات ٢٠،٢

ومن ترقّب الموت لَهَا عن اللذّات ٢١،٢

ومن زهد في الدنيا هانت عليه المصيبات ٢٢،٢

من مات غريباً مات شهيدًا ٢٣،٢

من ٱعتزّ بالعبيد أذلّه الله ٢٤،٢

من غشّنا فليس منّا ٢٥،٢

من رمانا بالليل فليس منّا ٢٦،٢

١ ت: تضيف حديثا (من قتل دون دمه فهو شهيد). ٢ ك: حذف الحديث.

Those who are killed defending their property die martyrs. 2.13

Those who are killed defending their family die martyrs. 2.14

Those who are killed defending their faith die martyrs. 2.15

God afflicts those he wishes to bless. 2.16

God teaches knowledge of religious practice to those he wishes to bless. 2.17

God gives good character to those he wishes to bless. 2.18

Those who long for the garden hasten to perform good deeds. 2.19

Those who fear the fire are oblivious to desires. 2.20

Those who expect death are oblivious to ephemeral pleasures. 2.21

Those who renounce the world bear afflictions with serenity. 2.22

Those who die in a foreign land die martyrs. 2.23

God brings to their knees those who exult in many slaves.[51] 2.24

If you deceive us you are not one of us. 2.25

If you attack us at night you are not one of us. 2.26

من لم يأخذ شاربه فليس منّا ٢٧،٢

من أحدث في أمرنا هذا ما ليس منه فهو رَدٌّ ٢٨،٢

من تأنّى أصاب أو كاد ومن عَجِل أخطأ أو كاد ٢٩،٢

من يزرع خيرًا يحصد رغبة ومن يزرع شرًّا يحصد ندامة ٣٠،٢

من أيقن بالخَلَف جاد بالعطيّة ٣١،٢

من أحبّ أن يكون أكرم الناس فليتّق الله ٣٢،٢

ومن أحبّ أن يكون أقوى الناس فليتوكّل على الله ٣٣،٢

ومن أحبّ أن يكون أغنى الناس فليكن بما في يد الله أوثق منه بما في يده ٣٤،٢

من همّ بذنب ثمّ تركه كانت له حسنة ٣٥،٢

من آتاه الله خيرًا فليُرَ عليه ٣٦،٢

من سرّه أن يَسلم فليلزم الصمت ٣٧،٢

من كثر كلامه كثر سَقَطه ومن كثر سقطه كثرت ذنوبه ومن كثرت ذنوبه كانت النار أولى به ٣٨،٢

من رُزق من شيئ فليلزمه ٣٩،٢

من أُزلّت إليه نعمةٌ فليشكرها ٤٠،٢

If you do not trim your mustache you are not one of us.[52] 2.27

Those who introduce innovations into our faith are to be rebuffed. 2.28

Those who deliberate may hit the mark, those who rush may miss the mark. 2.29

Those who sow good reap felicity, those who sow evil reap remorse. 2.30

Those who are certain about the hereafter give generously. 2.31

Those who wish to be noblest should remain devoted to God. 2.32

Those who wish to be strongest should trust in God. 2.33

Those who wish to be richest should rely on what God has more than on what they have. 2.34

Those who are tempted to sin but refrain earn a reward. 2.35

Those whom God has favored should show it. 2.36

Those who wish to remain safe should remain silent. 2.37

Those who talk a lot err a lot, those who err a lot sin a lot, and those who sin a lot are well suited to the fire. 2.38

Those given a means of sustenance should adhere to it. 2.39

Those granted a favor should be grateful. 2.40

من لم يشكر القليل لم يشكر الكثير ٢،٤١

من عزّى مصاباً فله مثل أجره ٢،٤٢

من فطّر صائماً كان له مثل أجره ٢،٤٣

من رفق بأمّتي رفق الله به ٢،٤٤

من عاد مريضاً لم يزل في خُرْفة الجنّة ٢،٤٥

من دعا على من ظلمه فقد ٱنتصر ٢،٤٦

من مشى مع ظالم فقد أجرم ٢،٤٧

من تشبّه بقوم فهو منهم ٢،٤٨

من طلب العلم تكفّل الله برزقه ٢،٤٩

من لم ينفعه علمه ضرّه جهله ٢،٥٠

من أبطأ به عمله لم يُسرع به نسبه ٢،٥١

من جُعل قاضياً فقد ذُبح بغير سكّين ٢،٥٢

من حَمل سِلعته فقد برئ من الكبر ٢،٥٣

من يُشادَّ هذا الدين يغلبه ٢،٥٤

من كذّب بالشفاعة لم ينلها يوم القيامة ٢،٥٥

Ungrateful for a little, ungrateful for a lot. 2.41

Those who console the afflicted will be recompensed in like measure. 2.42

Those who feed a person breaking fast will be recompensed in like measure. 2.43

God will be kind to those who are kind to my community. 2.44

Those who visit the sick will enjoy the fruits of the garden. 2.45

To pray against an oppressor is to have your wish granted. 2.46

To walk with tyrants is to commit a crime. 2.47

To emulate a group of people is to become one of them. 2.48

God provides sustenance for those who seek knowledge. 2.49

Those who do not benefit from their knowledge are harmed by their ignorance. 2.50

Those who are held back by their deeds are not urged on by their lineage. 2.51

To be appointed judge is to be slaughtered without a knife. 2.52

To transport your own goods is to be saved from arrogance. 2.53

Those who overburden themselves with their faith will find it overwhelms them. 2.54

On judgment day, those who discredit intercession will be denied it. 2.55

من سرّته حسنته وساءته سيّئته فهو مؤمن ٥٦،٢

من صام الأبد فلا صام ٥٧،٢

من خاف أدلج ومن أدلج بلغ المنزل ٥٨،٢

من يشتهِ كرامة الآخرة يدع زينة الدنيا ٥٩،٢

من كثرت صلاته بالليل حسن وجهه بالنهار ٦٠،٢

من أحبّ دنياه أضرّ بآخرته ومن أحبّ آخرته أضرّ بدنياه ٦١،٢

من أهان سلطان الله أهانه الله ومن أكرم سلطان الله أكرمه الله ٦٢،٢

من أحبّ عمل قوم خيرًا كان أو شرًّا كمن عمله ٦٣،٢

من ٱستعاذكم بالله فأعيذوه ومن سألكم بالله فأعطوه ومن دعاكم فأجيبوه ومن أتى إليكم معروفًا فكافئوه فإن لم تجدوا فٱدعوا له حتّى تعلموا أنّكم قد كافأتموه ٦٤،٢

من مشى منكم إلى طمع فليمش رويدًا ٦٥،٢

من عمّره الله ستّين سنة فقد أعذر إليه[١] ٦٦،٢

من أصبح لا ينوي ظلم أحد غُفر له ما جنى ٦٧،٢

من ألقى جلباب الحياء فلا غيبة له ٦٨،٢

---

١ ظ، م، ت: تضيف في إحدى رواياتها: (في العمر).

Those who are pleased by good deeds and pained by bad ones are true believers. 2.56

Those who fast continually have not fasted at all.[53] 2.57

Those who fear are cautious, and those who are cautious attain their goal. 2.58

Those who desire the glory of the hereafter forswear the vanities of this world. 2.59

The faces of those who pray much at night glow during the day. 2.60

Those who love worldly things are heedless of the hereafter. Those who love the hereafter are heedless of worldly things. 2.61

God denigrates those who denigrate his authority and honors those who honor it. 2.62

Approving of someone's deeds, good or evil, is the same as doing them. 2.63

If someone asks you for help in God's name, give it. If someone asks you for something in God's name, grant it. If someone gives you an invitation, accept it. If someone does you a good deed, give good in return, and if you do not have the wherewithal, pray for him until you know you have compensated him. 2.64

Proceed slowly toward your ambitions. 2.65

Anyone whom God has granted sixty years of life has no excuse. 2.66

God forgives the lapses of those who wake up intending no one harm. 2.67

You cannot be guilty of slandering the shameless. 2.68

من ساءته خطيئته غُفر له وإن لم يستغفر ٦٩،٢

من خاف الله خوّف الله منه كلّ شيء ومن لم يخف الله خوّفه الله من كلّ شيء ٧٠،٢

من أحبّ لقاء الله أحبّ الله لقاءه ومن كره لقاء الله كره الله لقاءه ٧١،٢

من سئل عن علم يعلمه فكتمه أُلجم بلجام من نار ٧٢،٢

من ٱستطاع منكم أن تكون له خبيئة من عمل صالح فليفعل ٧٣،٢

من فُتح له باب خير فلينتهزه فإنّه لا يدري متى يغلق عنه ٧٤،٢

من كظم غيظًا وهو يقدر على إنفاذه ملأه الله أمنًا وإيمانًا ٧٥،٢

من سرّه أن يجد طعم الإيمان فليحبّ المرء لا يحبّه إلّا لله تعالى ٧٦،٢

من أصاب مالًا من نَهَاوِش أذهبه الله في نَهَابِر ٧٧،٢

من أعطي حظّه من الرفق فقد أعطي حظّه من خير الدنيا والآخرة[١] ٧٨،٢

من آثر محبّة الله على محبّة الناس كفاه الله مؤونة الناس ٧٩،٢

من فارق الجماعة شِبرًا خلع رِبقة الإسلام من عنقه ٨٠،٢

من فارق الجماعة وٱستذلّ الإمارة لقي الله ولا وجه له عنده ٨١،٢

---

١ ظ، م: رواية إضافيّة (. . . من الخير). تضيف ت، م هنا حديثا: (إنّ الله يبغض الفاحش البذيّ).

Transgressions that the transgressor is sorry for will be forgiven even if he does not ask for forgiveness. 2.69

He who fears God is feared by everyone, and he who does not, fears everything. 2.70

God longs to meet those who long to meet him. God has no wish to meet those who have no wish to meet him. 2.71

Those who conceal what they know when asked about something will wear a bridle of fire. 2.72

Set aside a secret store of good deeds if you can. 2.73

Take advantage of any opportunity to do good, for you do not know when that door will close. 2.74

God fills with belief and a sense of security those who curb rage when they could act upon it. 2.75

To savor true belief, you should love people only for the sake of God. 2.76

God will cast into the abyss those who gain wealth through rapine. 2.77

To be granted a share of gentleness is to be granted a share of good in this world and the next. 2.78

God takes such care of those who prefer his love to the love of people that they have no need of charity. 2.79

To distance yourself from the community by even a handspan is to remove the halter of Islam from your neck. 2.80

When those who distance themselves from the community and denigrate its leadership meet God, they will be refused his regard. 2.81

من نزع يده من الطاعة لم تكن له يوم القيامة حجّة ٨٢،٢

ومن فارق الجماعة مات ميتة جاهليّة ٨٣،٢

من سرّه أن يسكن بُحبْوحة الجنّة فليلزم الجماعة ٨٤،٢

من أقال نادماً بَيعته أقاله الله تعالى عثرته[١] ٨٥،٢

من كفّ لسانه عن أعراض الناس أقاله الله تعالى عثرته يوم القيامة ٨٦،٢

من فرّق بين والدة وولدها فرّق الله بينه وبين أحِبّته يوم القيامة ٨٧،٢

من شاب شيبة في الإسلام كانت له نوراً يوم القيامة ٨٨،٢

من يسّر على معسر يسّر الله عليه في الدنيا والآخرة ٨٩،٢

من أنظر معسراً أو وضع له أظلّه الله تحت ظلّ عرشه يوم لا ظلّ إلّا ظلّه ٩٠،٢

من كان ذا لسانين في الدنيا جُعل له يوم القيامة لسانان من نار ٩١،٢

من نظر في كتاب أخيه بغير إذنه فكأنّما ينظر في النار ٩٢،٢

---

١ ظ: رواية إضافيّة (من أقال نادمًا أقاله الله عثرته يوم القيامة).

Those who refuse to fulfill the pledge of obedience will have no excuse on judgment day. 2.82

To leave the community is to die a pagan death. 2.83

If you wish to dwell in the center of the garden you should cleave to the community. 2.84

God will forgive the lapses of those who accept returned goods. 2.85

On judgment day, God will forgive the lapses of those who do not attack the good name of others. 2.86

Those who separate mother from child will be separated from their loved ones on judgment day. 2.87

On judgment day, the white hair of those who grow old obeying God will turn to light. 2.88

In this world and the next, God will ease the lot of those who ease the lot of someone in penury. 2.89

On a day when the only shade is his, God will shelter beneath his throne those who grant a delay or write off the debt of a person in penury. 2.90

Those who are two-tongued in this world will be given two tongues of fire on judgment day. 2.91

Those who peer at their brother's correspondence without permission peer into the fire. 2.92

من كان آمرًا بمعروف فليكن أمره ذلك بمعروف ٩٣،٢

من أخلص لله أربعين صباحاً ظهرت ينابيع الحكمة من قلبه على لسانه ٩٤،٢

من كان يؤمن بالله واليوم الآخر فليكرم ضيفه ٩٥،٢

ومن كان يؤمن بالله واليوم الآخر فليكرم جاره ٩٦،٢

ومن كان يؤمن بالله واليوم الآخر فليقل خيرًا أو ليصمت ٩٧،٢

من أسلم على يديه رجل وجبت له الجنّة ٩٨،٢

من نصر أخاه بظهر الغيب نصره الله في الدنيا والآخرة ٩٩،٢

من فرّج عن أخيه كربة من كرب الدينا فرّج الله عنه كربة من كرب يوم القيامة ١٠٠،٢

ومن كان في حاجة أخيه كان الله في حاجته ١٠١،٢

ومن ستر على أخيه ستره الله في الدنيا والآخرة ١٠٢،٢

والله في عون العبد ما كان العبد في عون أخيه ١٠٣،٢

من بنى لله مسجدًا ولو مثل مفحص قَطاة بنى الله له بيتاً في الجنّة ١٠٤،٢

Command good with gentleness. 2.93

The wellsprings of wisdom will flow from the heart to the tongue of those who for forty mornings devote themselves completely to God. 2.94

Those who believe in God and the last day should honor their guests. 2.95

Those who believe in God and the last day should honor their neighbors. 2.96

Those who believe in God and the last day should say only good things or keep silent. 2.97

Paradise is guaranteed to those who guide others to accept Islam. 2.98

In this world and the next, God will safeguard those who safeguard a brother in his absence. 2.99

On judgment day, God will deliver from hardship those who deliver a brother from hardship in this world. 2.100

God will come to the aid of those who come to their brother's aid. 2.101

In this world and the next, God will conceal the faults of those who conceal their brother's faults. 2.102

God supports a man as long as he supports his brother. 2.103

God will build a house in paradise for those who build a mosque, even one as tiny as a bird's nest.[54] 2.104

من طلب علماً فأدركه كُتب له كِفْلان من الأجر ومن طلب علماً فلم يدركه كتب له كفل من الأجر ١٠٥،٢

من سمّع الناس بعمله سمّع الله به سامِعَ خلقه يوم القيامة وحقّره وصغّره ١٠٦،٢

من طلب عمل الدنيا بعمل الآخرة فما له في الآخرة من نصيب ١٠٧،٢

من أُولي معروفاً فلم يجد جزاء إلّا الثناء فقد شكره ومن كتمه فقد كفره ١٠٨،٢

من أُولي معروفاً فليكافئ به فإن لم يستطع فليذكره فإن ذكره فقد شكره ١٠٩،٢

من أولى رجلاً من بني عبد المطّلب معروفاً في الدنيا فلم يقدر أن يكافئه كافأتُه عنه يوم القيامة ١١٠،٢

من رأى عورة فسترها كان كمن أحيا مَوْؤُودَة من قبرها ١١١،٢

من ٱنقطع إلى الله كفاه الله كلّ مؤونة ورزقه من حيث لا يحتسب ومن ٱنقطع إلى الدنيا وكّله الله إليها ١١٢،٢

من طلب محامد الناس بمعاصي الله عاد حامده من الناس ذامّاً ١١٣،٢

من ٱلتمس رضى الله بسخط الناس رضي الله عنه وأرضى عنه الناس ومن ٱلتمس رضى الناس بسخط الله سخط الله عليه وأسخط عليه الناس ١١٤،٢

Those who seek and find knowledge get two rewards; those who seek but do not find it get one. 2.105

God will punish and humiliate those who boast of their good deeds by letting his creatures hear their boasts on judgment day. 2.106

Those who do good deeds only to receive worldly gain will receive no share of the hereafter. 2.107

Those who praise an act of generosity have shown gratitude; those who keep silent are ingrates. 2.108

Generosity should be requited. If it cannot be requited, it should be spoken of—to speak of it is to show gratitude for it. 2.109

On judgment day, I shall requite any unrequited act of generosity to a member of the ʿAbd al-Muṭṭalib clan.[55] 2.110

To see someone's shame and conceal it is like bringing a buried girl back to life.[56] 2.111

God will take complete care of those who devote themselves to God by sustaining them in ways they never imagined. God gives over to this world those who devote themselves to it. 2.112

Those who seek praise from their fellows by disobeying God will receive only their derision. 2.113

If you displease others by seeking to please God, then God will be pleased with you and will make others pleased with you. If you displease God by seeking to please others, then God will be displeased with you and will make others displeased with you. 2.114

من مات على خير عمله فٱرجوا له خيرًا ومن مات على سيّئ عمله فخافوا عليه ولا تيأسوا ٢،١١٥

من أذنب في الدنيا ذنبًا فعوقب به فالله أعدل من أن يثنّي عقوبته على عبده ومن أذنب ذنبًا فستره الله عليه وعفا عنه في الدنيا فالله أكرم من أن يعود في شيء قد عفا عنه ٢،١١٦

من لم يكن له ورع يصدّه عن معصية الله إذا خلا لم يعبأ الله بشيء من عمله ٢،١١٧

من أحسن صلاته حين يراه الناس ثمّ أساءها حين يخلو فتلك ٱستهانة ٱستهان بها ربّه ٢،١١٨

من لم تَنْهَهُ صلاتُه عن الفحشاء والمنكر لم يزدد بها من الله إلّا بعدًا ٢،١١٩

من حاول أمرًا بمعصية كان أفوَت لما رجا وأقرب لمجيء ما ٱتّقى ٢،١٢٠

من كانت له سريرة صالحة أو سيّئة نشر الله عليه منها رداء يُعرف به ٢،١٢١

من حلف على يمين فرآى خيرًا منها فليكفّر عن يمينه ثمّ ليفعل الذي هو خير ٢،١٢٢

من ٱبتلي من هذه البنات بشيء فأحسن إليهنّ كنّ له سترًا من النار ٢،١٢٣

من قتل عصفورًا عبثًا جاء يوم القيامة وله صُراخ عند العرش يقول ربّ سل هذا فيمَ قتلني في غير منفعة ٢،١٢٤

Expect someone who dies doing good to receive good. Fear but do not despair for someone who dies doing evil. 2.115

God is too just to punish a second time servants who commit a sin in this world and are punished here. And he is too generous to reverse judgment on a sin he has concealed and forgiven in this world. 2.116

God will give no weight to good deeds performed in public by those who disobey him in private. 2.117

To pray beautifully when people are present and to pray defectively in private is to scorn the lord with your prayer. 2.118

The ritual-prayer gains you nothing from God but greater distance if it does not restrain you from indecency and misdeeds.[57] 2.119

If you seek something through a misdeed you are less likely to get what you desire and more likely to get what you dread. 2.120

If your heart conceals a wish, good or evil, God will clothe you in it and identify you by it. 2.121

If you swear an oath and realize there is something better, you should expiate your oath and do the better thing. 2.122

If you are tested with daughters and do well by them, you will be shielded from the fire. 2.123

If you kill a sparrow for no reason, it will come to God's throne on judgment day, screaming, "Lord, ask this man: Why did he kill me for no reason?" 2.124

من سأل الناس أموالهم تكثّراً فإنّما هي جمر فليستقلّ منه أو ليستكثر ١٢٥،٢

من سأل عن ظهر غنًى فصداع في الرأس وداء في البطن ١٢٦،٢

من مشى إلى طعام لم يدع إليه فقد دخل سارقاً وخرج مغيراً ١٢٧،٢

من كان وُصلة لأخيه المسلم إلى ذي سلطان في منهج برّ أو تيسير عسير أعانه الله على إجازة الصراط يوم تدحض فيه الأقدام ١٢٨،٢

من لعب بالنَّرْدَشير فهو كمن غمس يده في لحم الخنزير ودمه ١٢٩،٢

من نزل على قوم فلا يصومنّ تطوّعاً إلّا بإذنهم ١٣٠،٢

من انتهر صاحب بدعة ملأ الله قلبه أمناً وإيماناً ١٣١،٢

من أهان صاحب بدعة آمنه الله يوم الفزع الأكبر ١٣٢،٢

من أصبح معافًى في بدنه آمِناً في سربه عنده قوت يومه فكأنّما حيزت له الدنيا ١٣٣،٢

من ولي شيئاً من أمر المسلمين فأراد الله به خيراً جعل معه وزيراً صالحاً فإن نسي ذكّره وإن ذكر أعانه ١٣٤،٢

من عامل الناس فلم يظلمهم وحدّثهم فلم يكذبهم ووعدهم فلم يخلفهم فهو ممّن كملت ١٣٥،٢

To ask for money and hoard it is like picking up burning coal, whether you hoard a little or a lot. 2.125

If you ask and are not in need, you will be afflicted with headaches and stomach pains. 2.126

If you attend a meal uninvited, you go as a thief and leave as a plunderer. 2.127

On the day when every foot will slip, God will help across the bridge those who intercede with a ruler on behalf of their fellow Muslim for a worthy cause or to ease a hardship. 2.128

Gambling is like plunging your hand in the flesh and blood of swine. 2.129

Guests should perform voluntary fasts only with their hosts' permission. 2.130

God fills with security and belief the hearts of those who rebuke devisers of heresy. 2.131

On the day of terror, God grants security to those who condemn devisers of heresy. 2.132

To wake up safe and sound in your home, with enough food for the day, is as good as owning the world. 2.133

If God wishes to assist a Muslim in authority, he gives him a pious counselor who will remind him when he forgets and support him when he remembers. 2.134

If a man deals with people without oppression, speaks without lying, and does not break his pledges, then his virtue is complete and his sense of justice 2.135

مروّته وظهرت عدالته ووجبت أخوّته وحرمت غيبته

من حفظ ما بين لَحييه وما بين رجليه دخل الجنّة ١٣٦،٢

من كذب عليَّ متعمّدًا فليتبوّأ مقعده من النار ١٣٧،٢

من نزلت به فاقة فأنزلها بالناس لم تُكتب له ١٣٨،٢

evident. He is the sort of person they should cherish as a brother, and slandering him is forbidden.

Those who safeguard what is between their jaws and between their thighs enter the garden. **2.136**

Those who attribute something to me falsely will have a seat in the fire. **2.137**

Those who complain to others when struck with poverty will receive no reward. **2.138**

الباب الثالث

حُفّت الجنّة بالمكاره وحفّت النار بالشهوات ١،٣

وجبت محبّة الله على من أُغضب فحَلُم ٢،٣

بُعثت بجوامع الكَلِم ٣،٣

ونُصرت بالرعب ٤،٣

نُصرت بالصَّبا وأُهلكت عاد بالدَّبور ٥،٣

يعجب ربّك من الشابّ ليست له صَبْوَة ٦،٣

كما تكونون يولّى عليكم ٧،٣

يبعث الناس يوم القيامة على نيّاتهم ٨،٣

يبعث شاهد الزور يوم القيامة مولغًا لسانه في النار ٩،٣

رحم الله آمرأً أصلح من لسانه ١٠،٣

Chapter Three

The garden is surrounded by torments, the fire by delights. 3.1

God's love is assured for those who curb their anger when provoked. 3.2

I was sent with profound words. 3.3

I am aided by awe. 3.4

I was aided by the Ṣabā Wind, ʿĀd was destroyed by the Dabūr Wind.[58] 3.5

Your lord is pleased with the youth who shuns immature behavior. 3.6

You get the ruler you deserve. 3.7

On judgment day, people will be ranked according to the worth of their intentions. 3.8

On judgment day, false witnesses will be resurrected with their tongues in the fire. 3.9

May God shower mercy on the man who keeps his tongue chaste. 3.10

رحم الله عبداً قال فغَنِم أو سكت فسلم ١١،٣

رحم الله المتخلّلين من أمّتي في الوضوء والطعام ١٢،٣

أبى الله أن يرزق عبده المؤمن إلّا من حيث لا يعلم ١٣،٣

كاد الفقر يكون كفراً وكاد الحسد يغلب القدر ١٤،٣

خُصّ البلاء بمن عرف الناس وعاش فيهم من لم يعرفهم ١٥،٣

يُطبع المؤمن على كلّ خُلُق ليس الخيانة والكذب ١٦،٣

تبنون ما لا تسكنون وتجمعون ما لا تأكلون وتأملون ما لا تدركون ١٧،٣

كم من مستقبل يوماً لا يستكمله ومنتظر غداً لا يبلغه ١٨،٣

عجبتُ لغافل ولا يغفل عنه ١٩،٣

وعجبت لمؤمّل دنيا والموت يطلبه ٢٠،٣

وعجبت لضاحك مِلأَ فيه ولا يدري أ أرضى الله أم أسخطه ٢١،٣

يا عجباً كلّ العجب للمصدّق بدار الخلود وهو يسعى لدار الغرور ٢٢،٣

عجباً للمؤمن فوالله لا يقضي الله للمؤمن قضاء إلّا كان خيراً له ٢٣،٣

May God shower mercy on the servant who speaks and succeeds, or who stays silent and safe. 3.11

May God shower mercy on those in my community who clean their mouths during ablution and after meals. 3.12

God will grant believers sustenance only from unexpected sources.[59] 3.13

Poverty can almost be disbelief,[60] and envy can all but overpower destiny.[61] 3.14

Knowing a lot of people is toilsome, not knowing so many means a life of peace. 3.15

Treachery and lying are not among the traits of the believer. 3.16

You build what you shall not inhabit, you gather what you shall not eat, and you hope for what you shall not gain. 3.17

Many begin a day they will not complete, and await a morrow they will not attain. 3.18

I wonder at heedless men—they go not unheeded. 3.19

I wonder at men who seek worldly gains while death is seeking them out. 3.20

I wonder at men who laugh merrily, not knowing if they have pleased or angered God. 3.21

Those who acknowledge the abode of permanence yet strive for the abode of deception are a strange wonder indeed. 3.22

I wonder at believers—I swear God only ordains that which is good for them.[62] 3.23

اقتربت الساعة ولا يزداد الناس على الدنيا إلّا حرصاً ولا تزداد منهم إلّا بعداً ٢٤،٣

يهرم ابن آدم وتشبّ معه اثنتان الحرص على المال والحرص على العمر ٢٥،٣

جُبلت القلوب على حبّ مَن أحسن إليها وبغض من أساء إليها ٢٦،٣

جفّ القلم بالشقيّ والسعيد وفرغ الله من أربع من الخَلق والخُلق والأجَل والرزق ٢٧،٣

فرغ الله إلى كلّ عبد من خمس من عمله وأجَله وأثره ومضجعه ورزقه لا يتعدّاهنّ عبد ٢٨،٣

جفّ القلم بما أنت لاقٍ ٢٩،٣

تجدون من شرّ الناس ذا الوجهين الذي يأتي هؤلاء بوجه وهؤلاء بوجه ٣٠،٣

يذهب الصالحون أسلافاً الأوّل فالأوّل حتّى لا تبقى إلّا حُثالة كحثالة التمر والشعير ٣١،٣
لا يبالي الله بهم

يبصر أحدكم القذى في عين أخيه ويدع الجذع في عينه ٣٢،٣

كبرت خيانة أن تحدّث أخاك حديثاً هو لك به مصدّق وأنت له كاذب ٣٣،٣

كأنّ الحقّ فيها على غيرنا وجب وكأنّ الموت فيها على غيرنا كُتب وكأنّ الذي نشيع من ٣٤،٣
الأموات سَفْرٌ عمّا قليل إلينا عائدون نبوّئهم أجداثهم ونأكل تراثهم كأنّا مخلّدون بعدهم

The hour draws near, yet people become more and more greedy for this world, while it eludes their grasp more and more. 3.24

Men may age, yet two traits stay young: greed for wealth and greed for life. 3.25

Hearts are conditioned to love those who are kind to them and to hate those who are cruel. 3.26

For both the wretched and the blissful the pen has stopped writing. God has decreed four irrevocable things: form, character, lifespan, and sustenance. 3.27

God has decreed five things his servant cannot escape: deeds, lifespan, reputation, final resting place, and sustenance. 3.28

The pen has written down everything you will confront. 3.29

The worst people are the two-faced, showing one face here and another face there. 3.30

The pious will diminish, one generation after another, until only scraps and chaff remain—and God will pay them no heed. 3.31

You spy the speck in your brother's eye, yet ignore the plank in your own.[63] 3.32

The worst form of treachery is to say to your brother something he believes to be true when you are actually lying. 3.33

We behave as though duties fall on others, not us, as though death is written for others, not us, as if the dead are travelers who will soon return. We carry 3.34

قد نسينا كلّ واعظة وأمِنّا كلّ جائحة

طوبى لمن شغله عيبه عن عيوب الناس وأنفق من مال اكتسبه من غير معصية وخالط أهل الفقه والحكمة وجانب أهل الذلّ والمعصية ٣،٣٥

طوبى لمن ذلّ في نفسه وحسنت خليقته وأنفق الفضل من ماله وأمسك الفضل من قوله ووسعته السنّة ولم يَعْدُها إلى بدعة ٣،٣٦

طوبى[١] لمن هُدي للإسلام وكان عيشه كفافا وقنع به ٣،٣٧

طوبى لمن طاب كسبه وصلحت سريرته وكرمت علانيته وعزل عن الناس شرّه ٣،٣٨

طوبى لمن عمل بعلمه ٣،٣٩

ابنَ آدم عندك ما يكفيك وأنت تطلب ما يُطغيك ٣،٤٠

ابن آدم لا بقليل تقنع ولا من كثير تشبع ٣،٤١

---

١ ت، م: رواية إضافيّة: (أفلح من هدي للإسلام . . .).

their bodies to the grave and consume their wealth as though we will live forever. We forget all counsel and ignore every catastrophe.

Blessed are those whose own faults distract them from the faults of others, who spend their wealth without disobeying God, who associate with sensible and wise people, and who shun the depraved and sinful. 3.35

Blessed are those who possess humble hearts and beautiful character, who spend surplus wealth and suppress needless words, and who find that our established practice gives them enough latitude not to transgress into heresy. 3.36

Blessed are those guided to Islam who live a simple life of contentment. 3.37

Blessed are those who earn an honest living, whose hearts are pure, whose actions are noble, and from whom no one need fear any evil. 3.38

Blessed are those who act on their knowledge. 3.39

Son of Adam, you have all you need—why do you seek that which will make you a tyrant? 3.40

Son of Adam, you are neither content with a little nor sated by a lot! 3.41

الباب الرابع

اشفعوا تؤجروا ١،٤

سافروا تصحّوا وتغنموا ٢،٤

يسّروا ولا تعسّروا وسكّنوا ولا تنفّروا ٣،٤

قاربوا وسدّدوا ٤،٤

زُرْ غِبّاً تزدد حبّاً ٥،٤

قَيِّدْها وتوكّل ٦،٤

ابدأ بمن تعول ٧،٤

أُخْبُرْ تَقْلِهْ وثِقْ بالناس رويداً ٨،٤

قيّدوا العلم بالكتاب ٩،٤

أقلّ من الدَّين تعش حرّاً وأقلّ من الذنوب يهن عليك الموت ١٠،٤

وانظر في أيّ نِصاب تضع ولدك فإنّ العِرق دسّاس ١١،٤

كن وَرِعاً تكن أَعْبَدَ الناس وكن قنعاً تكن أشكر الناس ١٢،٤

Chapter Four

Conciliate and be rewarded. 4.1

Travel and find health and wealth. 4.2

Be mild, not harsh. Inspire calm, not panic. 4.3

Draw people close and guide them aright. 4.4

Visit from time to time and affection will increase. 4.5

Tie up your camel and trust in God.[64] 4.6

Charity begins at home. 4.7

Test people and you will come to hate them—be slow to trust. 4.8

Secure knowledge by writing it down. 4.9

Lessen your burden of debt and you will live free. Lessen your burden of sin and you will be less terrified of death. 4.10

Careful where you sow your seed—what you reap might be poisoned.[65] 4.11

Abstain from immorality and you will be the best worshipper. Be content and you will be the most grateful. 4.12

وأحبب للناس ما تحبّ لنفسك تكن مؤمناً وأحسن مجاورة من جاورك تكن مسلماً ١٣،٤

أبا هِرٍّ أحسن جوار من جاورك تكن مسلماً وأحسن مصاحبة من صاحبك تكن مؤمناً وٱعمل بفرائض الله تكن عابداً وٱرض بقَسْم الله تكن زاهداً ١٤،٤

ازهد في الدنيا يحبك الله وٱزهد فيما في أيدي الناس يحبك الناس ١٥،٤

كن في الدنيا كأنّك غريب أو كأنّك عابر سبيل وعُدّ نفسك في أصحاب القبور ١٦،٤

دع ما يريبك إلى ما لا يريبك ١٧،٤

انصر أخاك ظالماً أو مظلوماً ١٨،٤

ارحم من في الأرض يرحمك من في السماء ١٩،٤

اسمح يسمح لك ٢٠،٤

وسلّم على أهل بيتك يكثر خير بيتك ٢١،٤

اسبغ الوضوء يزد في عمرك ٢٢،٤

وٱستعفف عن السؤال ما ٱستطعت ٢٣،٤

قل الحقّ وإن كان مرّاً ٢٤،٤

Wish for others what you wish for yourself and you will be a true believer. Be a good neighbor to those around you and you will be a true Muslim. 4.13

Be a good neighbor to those around you and you will be a true Muslim.[66] Be a good companion to those who walk with you and you will be a true believer. Do what God has mandated and you will be a true worshipper. Be content with the share God has allotted you and you will truly be indifferent to the world. 4.14

Be indifferent to the world and God will love you. Be indifferent to the possessions of others and they will love you. 4.15

Live in this world as an exile or a passerby, and think of yourself as dead and buried. 4.16

Forswear what causes doubt for what does not. 4.17

Help your brother both when he oppresses and when he is oppressed.[67] 4.18

Show compassion to your fellow humans on earth, and those in heaven will show you compassion. 4.19

Be kind to others and you will receive kindness. 4.20

Greet your family and its prosperity will increase. 4.21

Perform ablutions with care and live long. 4.22

Do not beg if you can avoid it. 4.23

Speak the truth even when it's bitter. 4.24

اتقّ الله حيث كنت ٢٥،٤

وأتبع السيّئة الحسنة تمحها ٢٦،٤

وخالِق الناس بخلق حسن ٢٧،٤

بُلّوا أرحامكم ولو بالسلام ٢٨،٤

تهادَوا تزدادوا حبّاً ٢٩،٤

وهاجروا تورثوا أبناءكم مجداً ٣٠،٤

وأقيلوا الكرام عثراتهم ٣١،٤

تهادوا فإنّ الهديّة تذهب وَحَر الصدر ٣٢،٤

اطلبوا الخير عند حِسان الوجوه ٣٣،٤

تهادوا بينكم فإنّ الهديّة تذهب بالسخيمة ٣٤،٤

تهادوا تحابّوا ٣٥،٤

تهادوا فإنّه يضعّف الحبّ ويذهب بغوائل الصدر ٣٦،٤

تهادوا فإنّ الهديّة تذهب بالضغائن ٣٧،٤

بلّغوا عنّي ولو آية ٣٨،٤

وحدّثوا عن بني إسرائيل ولا حرج ٣٩،٤

Remain conscious of God at all times. 4.25

Erase a bad deed with a good deed. 4.26

Be kind and respect people. 4.27

Show concern for your relatives, even with a greeting. 4.28

Giving gifts increases affection. 4.29

Emigrating bequeaths honor to your children.[68] 4.30

Forgive the noble their errors. 4.31

Give each other gifts—gifts remove rancor from the heart. 4.32

Seek goodness among the comely. 4.33

Give each other gifts—gifts remove hatred. 4.34

Give each other gifts and affection will grow. 4.35

Give each other gifts—gifts multiply affection and erase resentments. 4.36

Give each other gifts—gifts remove enmity. 4.37

Convey my message, even a single verse of the Qur'an. 4.38

Narrate the stories of the Jews, there is no harm in it. 4.39

اتّقوا فِراسة المؤمن فإنّه ينظر بنور الله تعالى ٤٠،٤

اتّقوا الحرام في البنيان فإنّه أساس الخراب ٤١،٤

أكرموا أولادكم وأحسنوا آدابهم ٤٢،٤

قولوا خيرًا تغنموا واْسكتوا عن شرّ تسلموا ٤٣،٤

تخيّروا لنطفكم ٤٤،٤

أكثروا من ذكر هادم اللذّات ٤٥،٤

روّحوا القلوب ساعة بساعة ٤٦،٤

اعتمّوا تزدادوا حلمًا ٤٧،٤

اعملوا فكلٌّ ميسّر لما خُلق له ٤٨،٤

تزوّجوا الوَدود الوَلود فإنّي مُكاثر بكم الأنبياء ٤٩،٤

تسحّروا فإنّ في السحور بركة ٥٠،٤

اتّقوا النار ولو بشقّ تمرة ٥١،٤

اتّقوا الشحّ فإنّ الشحّ[١] أهلك من كان قبلكم ٥٢،٤

استغنوا عن الناس ولو بشَوص السواك ٥٣،٤

أعْروا النساء يلزمن الحجال ٥٤،٤

---

١ ظ، ت، م: رواية إضافيّة (فإنّه).

Beware a believer's clairvoyance—he sees with God's light. 4.40

Beware an edifice built on unlawful gains—they are the foundation of its destruction. 4.41

Be generous with your children and teach them well. 4.42

Speak good words and you will reap a reward. Curb evil words and you will be safe. 4.43

Be careful where you put your seed. 4.44

Be ever mindful of death, the destroyer of pleasures.[69] 4.45

Pause from time to time.[70] 4.46

Wear a turban and your discernment will increase.[71] 4.47

Act, for the actions a person has been created to perform come naturally.[72] 4.48

Marry affectionate, fertile women, so I can boast of our abundance to other prophets. 4.49

Eat before dawn—the pre-dawn meal brings blessings.[73] 4.50

Avert the punishment of the fire, even with the gift of a date.[74] 4.51

Fear greed—it annihilated those who came before. 4.52

Avoid debt, even a used toothbrush.[75] 4.53

Strip women of finery and they will keep to the bridal pavilion.[76] 4.54

استوصوا بالنساء خيرًا فإنّهنّ عوانٍ عندكم ٥٥،٤

حصّنوا أموالكم بالزكاة ٥٦،٤

وداوُوا مرضاكم بالصدقة ٥٧،٤

وأعدّوا للبلاء الدعاء ٥٨،٤

اغتنموا الدعاء عند الرقّة فانّها رحمة ٥٩،٤

أَلِظّوا بيا ذا الجلال والإكرام ٦٠،٤

التمسوا الرزق في خبايا الأرض ٦١،٤

تفرّغوا من هموم الدنيا ما ٱستطعتم ٦٢،٤

كيلوا طعامكم يبارك لكم فيه ٦٣،٤

اطلبوا الفضل عند الرحماء من أمّتي تعيشوا في أكنافهم ٦٤،٤

اطلبوا الخير دهركم وتعرّضوا لنفحات رحمة الله فإنّ لله نفحات من رحمته يصيب بها من يشاء من عباده ٦٥،٤

اجمعوا وَضوءكم جمع الله شملكم ٦٦،٤

نوّروا بالفجر فإنّه أعظم للأجر ٦٧،٤

تمسّحوا بالأرض فإنّها بكم برّة ٦٨،٤

Be kind to women—they are ensconced in your homes. 4.55

Fortify your wealth by paying the alms-levy. 4.56

Heal the sick by giving charity. 4.57

Combat misfortune with prayer. 4.58

Pray when your heart is full—that is from God's mercy. 4.59

Pray repeatedly to the font of majesty and generosity. 4.60

Seek sustenance from what is hidden in the earth.[77] 4.61

Free yourself as much as possible from the cares of the world. 4.62

Measure out your grain and it will bring you blessings.[78] 4.63

Seek the generosity of the merciful in my community and live in their shelter. 4.64

Seek good your whole life and aspire to God's glorious gifts of mercy—he grants them to whomsoever he chooses. 4.65

Gather your water and God will gather your loved ones.[79] 4.66

To pray when the pre-dawn light has spread brings the greatest reward.[80] 4.67

Anoint yourself with earth—earth exudes compassion.[81] 4.68

دعوا الناس يرزق الله بعضهم من بعض ٦٩،٤

استعينوا على أموركم بالكتمان ٧٠،٤

استعينوا على إنجاح الحوائج بالكتمان لها ٧١،٤

التمسوا الجار قبل شراء الدار والرفيق قبل الطريق ٧٢،٤

تداوَوا فإنّ الذي أنزل الداء أنزل الدواء ٧٣،٤

أُحثوا في وجوه المدّاحين التراب ٧٤،٤

أحسنوا إذا وُلّيتم وآعفوا عمّا ملكتم ٧٥،٤

أطعموا طعامكم الأتقياء وأُوْلُوا معروفكم المؤمنين ٧٦،٤

استعيذوا بالله من طمع يهدي إلى طبَع ٧٧،٤

أجملوا في طلب الدنيا فإنّ كلاًّ ميسّر لما خُلق له منها ٧٨،٤

أصلحوا دنياكم وآعملوا لآخرتكم ٧٩،٤

أفشوا السلام تسلموا ٨٠،٤

أفشوا السلام وأطعموا الطعام وصلوا الأرحام وصلّوا بالليل والناس نيام تدخلوا الجنّة بسلام ٨١،٤

Let people be—God will sustain them through each other.[82] 4.69

Strengthen your affairs by concealing them. 4.70

Strengthen your chances of realizing your dreams by concealing them. 4.71

Size up a neighbor before buying a house, size up a companion before taking him on a journey. 4.72

Seek the cure—the one who created the illness created the cure. 4.73

Throw dirt in the face of flatterers. 4.74

Be kindly if you rule, and forgive your subjects their offenses. 4.75

Share your food with the pious and your wealth with believers. 4.76

Seek God's protection from greed—greed leads to disgrace. 4.77

Be moderate in seeking worldly things—they come naturally to those for whom they have been created. 4.78

Conduct your worldly affairs with integrity and work hard for the hereafter. 4.79

Call out the peace greeting and you will know peace. 4.80

Greet with peace, feed others, foster ties with kin, and pray at night when others sleep. Do this, and you will enter paradise in peace. 4.81

احفظوني في أصحابي فإنّهم خيار أمّتي ٨٢،٤

احفظوني في عترتي ٨٣،٤

استشيروا ذوي العقول ترشدوا ولا تعصوهم فتندموا ٨٤،٤

توبوا الى ربّكم من قبل أن تموتوا وبادروا بالأعمال الزاكية قبل أن تشغلوا وصلوا الذي بينكم وبينه بكثرة ذكركم إيّاه ٨٥،٤

تجافَوا عن عقوبة ذي المروءة ما لم يكن حدّاً ٨٦،٤

تجافوا عن ذنب السخيّ فإنّ الله آخذ بيده كلّما عثر ٨٧،٤

عودوا المريض واتّبعوا الجنائز تذكّركم الآخرة ٨٨،٤

ليكن بلاغ أحدكم من الدنيا زاد الراكب ٨٩،٤

اغتنم خمساً قبل خمس شبابك قبل هرمك وصحّتك قبل سقمك وغناك قبل فقرك وفراغك قبل شغلك وحياتك قبل موتك ٩٠،٤

ليأخذ العبد من نفسه لنفسه ومن دنياه لآخرته ومن الشبيبة قبل الكبر ومن الحياة قبل الممات فما بعد الدنيا من دار إلّا الجنّة أو النار ٩١،٤

Preserve my sanctity by honoring my companions, for they are the cream of my community. 4.82

Preserve my sanctity by honoring my progeny. 4.83

Seek advice from the intelligent and you will secure guidance. Ignore them and you will secure only regret. 4.84

Come to your lord in repentance before you die, hasten to perform virtuous deeds before you are distracted, and secure your link to him by always being mindful of him. 4.85

Recoil from punishing the honorable except for criminal acts.[83] 4.86

Avert your eyes when generous people sin—God grasps them by the hand each time they stumble. 4.87

Visit the sick and follow the funeral bier—they will remind you of the hereafter. 4.88

Be satisfied in this world with no more provisions than are needed for a journey. 4.89

Take advantage of five things before the arrival of five others: youth before old age, health before illness, wealth before poverty, leisure before occupation, and life before death. 4.90

All of God's servants should take advantage of life to better the soul, and of the world to obtain the hereafter. They should make the most of youth before old age, and of life before death—after this, the only home is paradise or hellfire. 4.91

كونوا في الدنيا أضيافاً ٩٢،٤

واتّخذوا المساجد بيوتاً ٩٣،٤

وعوّدوا قلوبكم الرقّة ٩٤،٤

وأكثروا التفكّر والبكاء ٩٥،٤

ولا تختلفنّ بكم الأهواء ٩٦،٤

أكرموا الشهود فإنّ الله يستخرج بهم الحقوق ويدفع بهم الظلم ٩٧،٤

اتّقوا دعوة المظلوم فإنّها تحمل على الغمام بقول الله تعالى وعزّتي وجلالي لأنصرنّك ولو بعد حين ٩٨،٤

ارحموا ثلاثة غنيّ قوم افتقر وعزيز قوم ذلّ وعالماً يلعب به الحمقى والجهّال ٩٩،٤

تعشّوا ولو بكفّ من حَشَف فإنّ ترك العَشاء مهرمة ١٠٠،٤

انظروا إلى من هو أسفل منكم ولا تنظروا إلى من هو فوقكم فإنّه أجدر أن لا تزدروا نعمة الله عليكم ١٠١،٤

أَمِط الأذى عن طريق المسلمين تكثر حسناتك ١٠٢،٤

أحبب حبيبك هوناً ما عسى أن يكون بغيضك يوماً ما وأبغض بغيضك هوناً ما عسى أن يكون حبيبك يوماً ما ١٠٣،٤

Live in this world as if you were a guest. 4.92

Make the mosque your home. 4.93

Train your heart to gentleness. 4.94

Meditate and weep often. 4.95

Do not follow your whims. 4.96

Honor witnesses—through them God protects your rights and dispels oppression. 4.97

Beware the prayer of the wronged—it is carried up to heaven by the clouds. For God says: I swear on my might and my glory, I will help you, even if you must wait a little. 4.98

Show compassion to three persons: a wealthy man who has been ruined, a powerful man who has been humbled, and a learned man mocked by fools and dullards. 4.99

Eat dinner, even if just a handful of dry dates—skipping dinner will age you. 4.100

Always look at the person who has less than you, not the one who has more, and you will value God's favors to you. 4.101

Remove harmful objects from a Muslim's path and you will be given ample reward. 4.102

Love your friend with some restraint, for the day may come when he is your enemy. Hate your enemy with some restraint, for the day may come when he is your friend. 4.103

أوصيك بتقوى الله فإنّه رأس أمرك ١٠٤،٤

وعليك بالجهاد فإنّه رهبانيّة أمّتي ١٠٥،٤

وَلْيَرُدَّكَ عن الناس ما تعرف من نفسك ١٠٦،٤

وٱخزن لسانك إلّا من خير فإنّك تغلب بذلك الشيطان ١٠٧،٤

اقرأ القرآن ما نهاك فإذا لم ينهك فلست تقرأه ١٠٨،٤

أدّ الأمانة إلى من ٱئتمنك ولا تخن من خانك ١٠٩،٤

أعطوا الأجير أجره قبل أن يجفّ عَرَقه ١١٠،٤

احفظ الله يحفظك ١١١،٤

احفظ الله تجده أمامك ١١٢،٤

تعرّف إلى الله في الرخاء يعرفك في الشدّة ١١٣،٤

وٱعلم أنّ ما أصابك لم يكن ليخطئك وما أخطأك لم يكن ليصيبك ١١٤،٤

وٱعلم أنّ الخلائق لو ٱجتمعوا أن يعطوك شيئاً لم يرد الله أن يعطيك لم يقدروا عليه أو يصرفوا عنك شيئاً أراد الله أن يصيبك به لم يقدروا على ذلك فإذا سألت فٱسأل الله وإذا ٱستعنت فٱستعن بالله وٱعلم أنّ النصر مع الصبر وأنّ الفرج مع الكرب وأنّ ١١٥،٤

I counsel you to be conscious of God—that is the pinnacle of faith. 4.104

Perform jihad—it is my community's time of monasticism. 4.105

Let what you know about yourself stop you from disparaging others. 4.106

Only let your tongue say good things—by doing this, you vanquish Satan. 4.107

Read the Qur'an only if you abide by its proscriptions—if you do not, you are not reading it at all. 4.108

Uphold the trust of those who give you something in trust, and do not breach the trust of those who breach yours. 4.109

Pay a worker before his sweat dries. 4.110

Hold fast to God's will and he will hold fast to you. 4.111

Hold fast to God's will and you will find him in front of you. 4.112

Invoke God in good times and he will remember you in hard times. 4.113

Know that whatever strikes you was never going to pass you by, and that whatever passes you by was never going to strike you. 4.114

Know that if the whole world were to come together to give you something God did not want you to have, they could not give it to you. And if they came together to deflect from you something God wanted to afflict you with, they could not. When you need to petition, petition God. When you need help, seek help from God. Victory comes with patience, deliverance comes after 4.115

﴿مَعَ ٱلْعُسْرِ يُسْرًا﴾ وٱعلم أنّ القلم قد جرى بما هو كائن

عش ما شئت فإنّك ميّت وأحبب من أحببت فإنّك مفارقه وٱعمل ما شئت فإنّك مجزيّ به ١١٦،٤

اصنع المعروف إلى من هو أهله وإلى من ليس أهله فإن أصبت أهله فهو أهله وإن لم تصب أهله فأنت من أهله ١١٧،٤

اشتدّي أزمةُ تنفرجي ١١٨،٤

أنفق يا بِلال ولا تخش من ذي العرش إقلالاً ١١٩،٤

بشّر المشّائين في ظلم الليل الى المساجد بالنور التامّ يوم القيامة ١٢٠،٤

عليك بذات الدين تَرِبَتْ يداك ١٢١،٤

عليكم من الأعمال بما تطيقون فإنّ الله لا يملّ حتّى تملّوا ١٢٢،٤

إذا وزنتم فأرجحوا ١٢٣،٤

إذا أتاكم كريم قوم فأكرموه ١٢٤،٤

إذا جاءكم الزائر فأكرموه ١٢٥،٤

إذا غضبت فٱسكت ١٢٦،٤

suffering, and «ease comes after hardship.»[84] Everything that is going to happen has already been recorded by the pen.

Live as you wish, you will surely die. Love whom you wish, you will surely leave them. Act as you wish, you will surely be paid back in kind. 4.116

Be generous to the worthy and unworthy alike. If your generosity falls on the worthy, good, they are worthy of it. If it falls on the unworthy, that is good too, for you are worthy of the act. 4.117

Do your worst, Calamity; you will soon dissipate. 4.118

Spend generously and do not fear poverty, for the lord of the throne will provide.[85] 4.119

Give glad tidings to those who walk to the mosque in the dark of night: on judgment day they will be illumined to perfection. 4.120

Marry a woman of faith—may your hands be filled with earth![86] 4.121

Do as many good deeds as you can—God will not tire till you tire. 4.122

Add a little extra when weighing out grain. 4.123

When those honored among their people come to you, honor them. 4.124

When visitors come to you, honor them. 4.125

Keep silent when roused to anger. 4.126

إذا أحبّ أحدكم أخاه فليُعلمه ١٢٧،٤

إذا بويع لخليفتين فاقتلوا الآخر منهما ١٢٨،٤

إذا تمنّى أحدكم فلينظر ما يتمنّى فإنّه لا يدري ما كُتب له من أمنيّته ١٢٩،٤

Tell your brother you love him. 4.127

When allegiance is given to two postulants, the second must be killed.[87] 4.128

Be careful what you wish for, you do not know where it will take you. 4.129

الباب الخامس

ما عال من ٱقتصد ١،٥

ما أعزّ الله بجهل قطّ ولا أذلّ الله بحلم قطّ ٢،٥

ما نُزعت الرحمة إلّا من شقيّ ٣،٥

ما شقي عبد قطّ بمشورة ولا سعد بٱستغناء برأي ٤،٥

ما خاب من ٱستخار ولا ندم من ٱستشار ولا عال من ٱقتصد ٥،٥

ما آمن بالقرآن من ٱستحلّ محارمه ٦،٥

ما رُزق العبد رزقًا أوسع عليه من الصبر ٧،٥

ما خالطت الصدقة مالاً إلّا أهلكته ٨،٥

ما نقص مال من صدقة ٩،٥

ولا عفى رجل عن مظلمة إلّا زاده الله بها عزًّا ١٠،٥

ما تركت بعدي فتنة أضرّ على الرجال من النساء ١١،٥

ما أصرّ من ٱستغفر ولو عاد في اليوم سبعين مرّة ١٢،٥

Chapter Five

Practice moderation and never know want. 5.1

God never honors harshness, nor demeans forbearance.[88] 5.2

Only the wretch is devoid of compassion. 5.3

No believer has ever suffered for soliciting an opinion, nor met with success by relying on his own. 5.4

Those who seek divine direction will not fail, those who seek good counsel will not regret, those who practice moderation will not want. 5.5

Anyone who permits what the Qur'an forbids does not believe in it. 5.6

There is no sustenance more sufficient for the believer than fortitude. 5.7

Failure to pay the alms-levy on one's wealth guarantees its destruction. 5.8

Giving alms never reduces wealth. 5.9

Whenever a man forgives a transgression, God increases his standing. 5.10

I do not leave you any temptation more injurious than women. 5.11

Even after seventy lapses a day, a penitent is still not a sinner. 5.12

ما أحسن عبد الصدقة إلّا أحسن الله الخلافة على تركته ١٣،٥

ما رأيت مثل النار نام هاربها ولا مثل الجنّة نام طالبها ١٤،٥

ما كان الرفق في شيء قطّ إلّا زانه وما كان الخُرق في شيء قطّ إلّا شانه ١٥،٥

ما ٱسترذل الله عبداً إلّا حظر عنه العلم والأدب ١٦،٥

ما أنزل الله من داء إلّا أنزل له شفاء ١٧،٥

ما زان الله عبداً بزينة أفضل من عفاف في دينه وفرجه ١٨،٥

ما عظمت نعمة الله على عبد إلّا عظمت مؤونة الناس عليه ١٩،٥

ما ستر الله على عبد في الدنيا ذنباً فيعيّره به يوم القيامة ٢٠،٥

ما أكرم شابّ شيخاً لسنّه إلّا قيّض الله له عند سنّه من يكرمه ٢١،٥

ما ٱمتلأت دار حبرة إلّا ٱمتلأت عبرة وما كانت فرحةٌ إلّا تبعتها ترحة ٢٢،٥

ما ٱسترعى الله عبداً رعيّة فلم يَحُطها بنصحه إلّا حرّم الله عليه الجنّة ٢٣،٥

ما من عبد يسترعيه الله رعيّة يموت يوم يموت غاشّاً لرعيّته إلّا حرّم الله عليه الجنّة ٢٤،٥

ما من رجل من المسلمين[١] أعظم أجرًا من وزير صالح مع إمام يطيعه ويأمره بذات الله تعالى ٢٥،٥

١ ت، م: رواية إضافية (ما من أحد من الناس)؛ ك: تضيف نسخة (ما أحد من الناس).

Whenever a believer gives alms in kindness, God watches over his children in kindness. 5.13

Those who flee the fire and those who seek the garden are never seen dozing. 5.14

Kindness always adorns, brutality always defiles. 5.15

God takes away the knowledge and manners of someone he means to demean. 5.16

God never sends an illness without sending its cure. 5.17

God graces his worshippers with nothing lovelier than chastity of belief and behavior. 5.18

As God's favors to his servants increase, their responsibility to others increase. 5.19

God does not conceal a servant's fault in this world only to shame him with it on judgment day. 5.20

When a youth shows respect to an elder because he is old, God ordains that people show him respect when he grows old. 5.21

Homes fill with happiness and then later with tears—joy is always followed by sorrow. 5.22

A person who neglects the flock God placed in his charge will be denied paradise. 5.23

A person who dies having deceived the flock God placed in his charge will be denied paradise. 5.24

No Muslim reaps greater reward than a virtuous counselor who obeys his leader and advises him for the sake of God. 5.25

ما من مؤمن إلّا وله ذنب يصيبه الفَينةَ بعد الفينة لا يفارقه حتّى يفارق الدنيا ٢٦،٥

ما طلعت شمس قطّ إلّا بجنبتيها ملكان يقولان اللّهم عجّل لمنفق خلفاً وعجّل لممسك تلفاً ٢٧،٥

ما ذئبان ضاريان في زَريبة غنم بأسرع فيها من حبّ الشرف والمال في دين المرء المسلم ٢٨،٥

ما عُبد الله بشيء أفضل من فقه في الدين ٢٩،٥

ما من شيء أُطيع الله فيه بأعجل ثواباً من صلة الرحم وما من عمل يُعصى الله فيه بأعجل عقوبة من بغي ٣٠،٥

ما فتح رجل على نفسه باب مسألة إلّا فتح الله عليه باب فقر ٣١،٥

ما ينتظر أحدكم من الدنيا إلّا غنًى مطغياً أو فقراً منسياً أو مرضاً مفسداً أو هرماً مفنداً أو موتاً مجهزاً ٣٢،٥

ما يصيب المؤمن وصَب ولا نصب ولا سقم ولا أذًى ولا حزن حتّى الهمّ يهمّه إلّا كفّر الله به من خطاياه ٣٣،٥

ما تزال المسألة بالعبد حتّى يلقى الله وما في وجهه مُزعة[١] ٣٤،٥

١ ك: تضيف نسخة (مُزعة لحم).

Every believer has at least one sin he keeps coming back to, time after time, only stopping when he leaves the world. 5.26

The sun as it rises is accompanied by an angel at each side saying, "God, grant swift reward to those who spend their wealth well, and swift destruction to those who hold it back." 5.27

Two hungry wolves do not wreak as much havoc in a flock of sheep as love of glory and wealth do to a Muslim's faith. 5.28

A good grasp of religion is how God is best worshipped. 5.29

No deed of obedience to God brings swifter reward than fostering affection with kin. No deed of disobedience brings swifter punishment than injustice. 5.30

Whenever someone opens the door to begging, God opens the door to penury. 5.31

Expect from the world nothing but wealth that oppresses, poverty that distracts, disease that corrupts, old age that debilitates, and death that crushes. 5.32

Whenever hunger, fatigue, illness, injury, grief, or even anxiety strike a believer, God erases his sins. 5.33

Beggars will meet God with their faces picked bare of flesh. 5.34

الباب السادس

لا يُلدغ المؤمن من جُحر مرّتين ١،٦

لا يشكر الله من لا يشكر الناس ٢،٦

لا يردّ القضاء إلّا الدعاء ولا يزيد في العمر إلّا البرّ ٣،٦

لا حليم إلّا ذو عثرة ولا حكيم إلّا ذو تجربة ٤،٦

لا فقر أشدّ من الجهل ٥،٦

ولا مال أعود من العقل ٦،٦

ولا وحدة أوحش من العجب ٧،٦

ولا مظاهرة أوثق من المشاورة ٨،٦

ولا عقل كالتدبير ٩،٦

ولا حسب كحسن الخلق ١٠،٦

ولا ورع كالكفّ ١١،٦

ولا عبادة كالتفكّر[١] ١٢،٦

ولا إيمان كالحياء والصبر ١٣،٦

١ ظ: رواية إضافيّة (لا عبادة أفضل من التفكّر).

Chapter Six

No believer is stung by the same snake twice.[89] 6.1

Ingratitude to others is ingratitude to God. 6.2

Nothing repels fate like prayer, nothing increases life like virtue.[90] 6.3

No one becomes prudent without stumbling, no one becomes wise without experience. 6.4

There is no poverty more intense than ignorance. 6.5

There is no wealth more useful than intelligence. 6.6

There is no solitude more antisocial than conceit. 6.7

There is no support more robust than consultation. 6.8

There is no intelligence better than planning. 6.9

There is no lineage better than good character. 6.10

There is no restraint as successful as avoiding what is forbidden. 6.11

There is no worship better than reflection. 6.12

There is no faith better than modesty and forbearance. 6.13

لا يُتْمَ بعد حُلُم ٦،١٤

لا حلف في الإسلام ٦،١٥

لا صَرورة في الإسلام ٦،١٦

لا هجرة بعد الفتح ٦،١٧

لا إيمان لمن لا أمانة له ٦،١٨

ولا دين لمن لا عهد له ٦،١٩

لا رُقية إلّا من عين أو حُمة ٦،٢٠

لا هجرة فوق ثلاث ٦،٢١

لا كبيرة مع ٱستغفار ولا صغيرة مع إصرار ٦،٢٢

لا همّ إلّا همّ الدَّين ولا وجع إلّا وجع العين ٦،٢٣

لا فاقة لعبد يقرأ القرآن ولا غنى له بعده ٦،٢٤

لا ينتطح فيها عنزان ٦،٢٥

لا يغني حذر من قدر ٦،٢٦

لا يفتك مؤمن ٦،٢٧

There is no orphancy after puberty. 6.14

There is no factionalism in Islam. 6.15

There is no bachelorhood in Islam.[91] 6.16

There is no emigration after the conquest.[92] 6.17

There is no belief without fidelity. 6.18

There is no faith without a covenant. 6.19

Amulets are only effective against the evil eye or the scorpion's sting. 6.20

No estrangement should persist more than three days. 6.21

No sin is grave if repented; no sin is small if repeated. 6.22

There is no worry worse than debt, no pain worse than sore eyes. 6.23

There is no poverty for those who recite the Qur'an, no wealth for those who do not. 6.24

No goats lock horns over her.[93] 6.25

No precaution can avert fate. 6.26

A believer does not kill. 6.27

لا يفلح قوم تملكهم ٱمرأة ٦،٢٨

لا ينبغي لمؤمن أن يُذلّ نفسه ٦،٢٩

لا ينبغي للصِّدّيق أن يكون لعّانًا ٦،٣٠

لا ينبغي لذي الوجهين أن يكون أميناً عند الله ٦،٣١

لا يصلح الملق إلّا للوالدين والإمام العادل ٦،٣٢

لا تصلح الصنيعة إلّا عند ذي حسب أو دين كما لا تصلح الرياضة إلّا في النجيب ٦،٣٣

لا طاعة لمخلوق في معصية الخالق ٦،٣٤

لا يدخل الجنّة عبد لا يأمن جاره بوائقَه ٦،٣٥

لا يدخل الجنّة قتّات ٦،٣٦

لا يحلّ لمسلم أن يروّع مسلماً ٦،٣٧

لا يحلّ لٱمرئ أن يهجر أخاه فوق ثلاث ٦،٣٨

لا تحلّ الصدقة لغنيّ ولذي مِرّة قويّ ٦،٣٩

لا يهلك الناس حتّى يعذروا من أنفسهم ٦،٤٠

A woman cannot lead a group to success.[94] 6.28

A believer should not demean himself. 6.29

An upright man should not curse. 6.30

A two-faced man cannot receive God's trust. 6.31

Only parents and just leaders deserve adulation. 6.32

Only the noble and the faithful deserve favors; only thoroughbreds deserve to be trained. 6.33

Do not obey God's creatures if it means you will disobey God. 6.34

Those feared by their neighbors will not enter paradise. 6.35

Rumor-mongers will not enter paradise. 6.36

It is unlawful for a Muslim to terrorize another Muslim. 6.37

It is unlawful for a man to remain estranged from his brother more than three days. 6.38

It is unlawful for the strong and able or the wealthy to solicit alms. 6.39

People are only punished when they have committed many crimes.[95] 6.40

لا يستقيم إيمان عبد حتّى يستقيم قلبه ولا يستقيم قلبه حتّى يستقيم لسانه ٦،٤١

لا يؤمن عبد حتّى يحبّ لأخيه ما يحبّ لنفسه من الخير ٦،٤٢

لا يبلغ العبد حقيقة الإيمان حتّى يعلم أنّ ما أصابه لم يكن يخطئه وما أخطأه لم يكن يصيبه ٦،٤٣

لا يستكمل العبد الإيمان حتّى تكون فيه ثلاث خصال الإنفاق من الإقتار والإنصاف من نفسه وبذل السلام ٦،٤٤

لا يستكمل أحدكم حقيقة الإيمان حتّى يخزن لسانه ٦،٤٥

لا يرحم الله من لا يرحم الناس ٦،٤٦

لا يشبع عالم من علمه حتّى يكون منتهاه الجنّة ٦،٤٧

لا يشبع المؤمن دون جاره ٦،٤٨

لا يزداد الأمر إلّا شدّة ولا الدنيا إلّا إدباراً ولا الناس إلّا شحّاً ولا تقوم الساعة إلّا على شرار الناس ٦،٤٩

ولا مهديّ إلّا عيسى ٱبن مريم ٦،٥٠

لا تقوم الساعة حتّى يقلّ الرجال ويكثر النساء ٦،٥١

A person's belief is right only when his heart is right, and his heart is right only when his tongue is righteous. 6.41

A person is only a believer when he wants for his brother the good he wants for himself. 6.42

A person only attains true belief when he knows that what struck him was never going to pass him by and what passed him by was never going to strike him. 6.43

A person attains perfect belief only through three modes of conduct: spending when funds are low, reckoning his actions justly, and wholeheartedly wishing peace on others. 6.44

You will only attain perfect belief when you restrain your tongue. 6.45

God shows no mercy to those who show no mercy to others. 6.46

The man of learning only has his fill of learning when it is time for paradise. 6.47

No believer eats his fill while his neighbor goes hungry. 6.48

Things will get progressively worse, the world will turn its back on you more and more, and people will become more and more greedy. The hour will only afflict the most evil of people. 6.49

Jesus, the son of Mary, is the only messiah. 6.50

The hour will come when men are few and women many. 6.51

لا يأتي على الناس زمان إلّا والذي بعده شرّ منه[١] ٦،٥٢

لا يستر عبد عبداً في الدنيا إلّا ستره الله تعالى يوم القيامة ٦،٥٣

لا خير في صحبة من لا يرى لك من الحقّ مثل الذي ترى له ٦،٥٤

لا تذهب حبيبتا عبد فيصبر ويحتسب إلّا دخل الجنّة ٦،٥٥

لا يبلغ العبد أن يكون من المتّقين حتّى يدع ما لا بأس به حذراً لما به البأس ٦،٥٦

لا تزال طائفة من أمّتي على الحقّ ظاهرين حتّى يأتي أمر الله ٦،٥٧

لا تزال نفس الرجل معلّقة بدَينه حتّى يُقضى عنه ٦،٥٨

لا يزال العبد في صلاة ما ٱنتظر الصلاة ٦،٥٩

لا تُظهر الشماتة لأخيك فيعافيه الله ويبتليك ٦،٦٠

لا تسبّوا الدهر فإنّ الله هو الدهر ٦،٦١

لا تسبّوا السلطان فإنّه فَيء الله في أرضه ٦،٦٢

لا تسبّوا الأموات فتؤذوا الأحياء ٦،٦٣

لا تسبّوا الأموات فإنّهم قد أفضَوا إلى ما قدّموا ٦،٦٤

---

١ ت، م: حذف الحديث.

Every age will be worse than the one before. 6.52

On judgment day, God will conceal the faults of those who have concealed the faults of others. 6.53

There is no good in the companionship of a man who does not regard you the way you regard him. 6.54

Paradise is guaranteed to those who accept God's will and endure when they lose the precious gift of sight. 6.55

You can only become one of the virtuous if you forgo lawful things to guard against unlawful ones. 6.56

A faction from my community will uphold the truth until judgment day. 6.57

A man's soul is mortgaged to his debt until someone pays it off. 6.58

A man awaiting the ritual-prayer is already at prayer. 6.59

Do not gloat over your brother's misfortune lest God restore him to well-being and smite you instead. 6.60

Do not curse fate—God is fate. 6.61

Do not curse the ruler—he is God's shadow on earth. 6.62

Do not curse the dead or you will pain the living. 6.63

Do not curse the dead for they have been called to account. 6.64

لا يردّ الرجل هديّة أخيه فإن وجد فليكافئه ٦،٦٥

لا تمسح يدك بثوب من لا تكسوه[١] ٦،٦٦

لا تردّوا السائل ولو بِشِقّ تمرة ٦،٦٧

لا تغتابوا المسلمين ولا تتّبعوا عوراتهم ٦،٦٨

لا تخرقنّ على أحد سِترًا ٦،٦٩

لا تحقرنّ من المعروف شيئًا ٦،٧٠

لا تواعد أخاك موعدًا فتخلفه ٦،٧١

لا يتمنّيَنّ أحدكم الموت لضرّ نزل به ٦،٧٢

لا يموتنّ أحد[٢] إلّا وهو يحسن الظنّ بالله ٦،٧٣

لا تحاسدوا ولا تناجشوا ولا تباغضوا ولا تدابروا وكونوا عباد الله إخوانًا ٦،٧٤

لا تكونوا عيّابين ولا مدّاحين ولا طعّانين ولا متماوتين ٦،٧٥

لا تعجبوا بعمل عامل حتّى تنظروا بم يختم له ٦،٧٦

لا يعجبنّكم إسلام رجل حتّى تعلموا كُنْه عقله ٦،٧٧

لا تجعلوني كقَدَح الراكب ٦،٧٨

---

١ ك: (لا تكسوا) ولعلّ المراد (لا تكسو). ٢ م: (أحدكم)؛ ك: تثبت الروايتين.

Do not reject your brother's gift. If possible, reward him in kind. 6.65

Do not wipe your hand on the garment of someone you have not clothed.[96] 6.66

Do not refuse a beggar even half a date. 6.67

Do not slander fellow Muslims and do not seek to expose them. 6.68

Do not rend another's veil. 6.69

Do not belittle any form of charity. 6.70

Do not make a promise to your brother only to break it. 6.71

Do not wish for death when catastrophe strikes. 6.72

Approach death with trust in God's reward. 6.73

Do not envy each other, bid against each other, hate each other, or shun each other. Servants of God, regard each other as brothers. 6.74

Do not be slanderers, flatterers, mudslingers, or sham devotees. 6.75

Be impressed by a person's actions only when you see how they play out. 6.76

Be impressed by a man's adherence to Islam only when you know his true intentions. 6.77

Do not slight me as if I were an afterthought, a mere travel cup.[97] 6.78

لا تمنعنّ أحدكم مهابة الناس أن يقوم بالحقّ إذا علمه ٦،٧٩

لا يخلونّ رجل بٱمرأة فإنّ ثالثهما الشيطان ٦،٨٠

لا تُرضينّ أحدًا بسخط الله ولا تحمدنّ أحدًا على فضل الله ولا تذمّنّ أحدًا على ما لم يؤتك الله فإنّ رزق الله لا يسوقه إليك حرص حريص ولا يردّه عنك كراهية[١] كاره ٦،٨١

لا تسأل الإمارة فإنّك إن أُعطيتَها عن غير مسألة أُعِنت عليها وإن أعطيتها عن مسألة وُكّلت إليها ٦،٨٢

لا تقوم الساعة حتّى يكون الولد غيظًا والمطر قيظًا وتفيض اللئام فيضًا وتغيض الكرام غيضًا ويجترئ الصغير على الكبير واللئيم على الكريم ٦،٨٣

لن يهلك ٱمرؤ بعد مشورة ٦،٨٤

لن تهلك الرعيّة وإن كانت ظالمة مسيئة إذا كانت الولاة هادية مهديّة ٦،٨٥

فصل

إيّاك وما يُعتذر منه ٦،٨٦

إيّاكم والمدحَ فإنّه الذبح ٦،٨٧

إيّاك ومحقّرات الذنوب فإنّ لها من الله طالبًا ٦،٨٨

---

١ ك: (كراهة).

Do not let fear of others prevent you from standing up for the truth. 6.79

A man should never be alone with a woman—Satan will make it a threesome. 6.80

Do not displease God by pleasing others, do not praise them for God's favors, and do not blame them for having something God did not give you. Covetousness will not bring God's sustenance to you, nor will someone's hatred drive it away. 6.81

Do not seek leadership—God will help you if you are given it unbidden, but will leave you to your own devices if you sought it. 6.82

The hour will come when children are disobedient, when drought scorches the earth, when the contemptible inundate the land, when the noble are few, when the young are insolent to their elders, and the contemptible insolent to the noble. 6.83

No man will be ruined if he seeks counsel. 6.84

Even evil and oppressive people will not be ruined if their leaders are rightly guided and give good guidance. 6.85

Beware of an action that requires an apology. 6.86

Beware of flattery—it is a form of slaughter. 6.87

Beware the accumulation of little sins—God is keeping count. 6.88

إيّاك ومُشارّة الناس فإنّها تظهر العُرّة وتدفن الغُرّة ٦،٨٩

إيّاكم وخضراء الدِّمَن ٦،٩٠

إيّاكم والدَّين فإنّه همّ باللّيل ومذلّة بالنهار ٦،٩١

إيّاكم والظنّ فإنّ الظنّ أكذب الحديث ٦،٩٢

إيّاكم ودعوة المظلوم وإن كان كافرًا ٦،٩٣

Beware of heated dispute—it exposes bad behavior and stifles good conduct. 6.89

Beware of beautiful flowers growing in dung heaps.[98] 6.90

Beware of debt—it distresses at night and humiliates by day. 6.91

Beware of giving voice to suspicions—they are the falsest words. 6.92

Beware the prayer of the wronged, even an unbeliever's. 6.93

الباب السابع

إنّ من البيان سحرًا ١،٧

وإنّ من الشعر حكمًا ٢،٧

وإنّ من القول عِيالًا ٣،٧

وإنّ مِن طلب العلم جهلًا ٤،٧

إنّ أمّتي أمّة مرحومة ٥،٧

إنّ حسن العهد من الإيمان ٦،٧

إنّ حسن الظنّ من حسن العبادة ٧،٧

إنّ العلماء ورثة الأنبياء ٨،٧

إنّ الدين يسر ٩،٧

إنّ دين الله الحنيفيّة السمحة ١٠،٧

إنّ أعجل الطاعة ثوابًا صلة الرحم ١١،٧

إنّ الحكمة تزيد الشريف شرفًا ١٢،٧

Chapter Seven

From eloquence comes magic. 7.1

From poetry comes wisdom. 7.2

From speech comes distress.[99] 7.3

From the pursuit of knowledge comes ignorance.[100] 7.4

My community will receive mercy. 7.5

Maintaining relationships is part of faith.[101] 7.6

A good worshipper expects good of others. 7.7

The learned are the heirs of the prophets. 7.8

Religion is accommodating. 7.9

God's religion is moderate and righteous.[102] 7.10

Fostering ties with kin is the duty quickest to earn reward. 7.11

Wisdom increases the noble in nobility. 7.12

إنّ محرِّم الحلال كمُحِلّ الحرام ١٣،٧

إنّ أحساب أهل الدنيا هذا المال ١٤،٧

إنّ لصاحب الحقّ مقالاً ١٥،٧

إنّ مكارم الأخلاق من أعمال أهل الجنّة ١٦،٧

إنّ أحسن الحسن الخلق الحسن ١٧،٧

إنّ مولى القوم من أنفسهم ١٨،٧

إنّ أكثر أهل الجنّة البُلْه ١٩،٧

إنّ أقلّ ساكني الجنّة النساء ٢٠،٧

إنّ المعونة تأتي العبد من الله على قدر المؤونة ٢١،٧

وإنّ الصبر يأتي العبد على قدر المصيبة ٢٢،٧

إنّ أبرّ البرّ أن يصل الرجل أهل ودّ أبيه بعد أن يولّي الأب ٢٣،٧

إنّ الشيطان يجري من ٱبن آدم مجرى الدم ٢٤،٧

إنّ أشكر الناس لله أشكرهم للناس ٢٥،٧

إنّ إعطاء هذا المال فتنة وإمساكه فتنة ٢٦،٧

إنّ عذاب هذه الأمّة جُعل في دنياها ٢٧،٧

Declaring the lawful unlawful is akin to declaring the unlawful lawful. 7.13

In the eyes of the worldly, nobility comes from wealth. 7.14

Honest claimants have a right to speak. 7.15

The dwellers of paradise are characterized by virtuous conduct. 7.16

The loveliest beauty is beauty of character. 7.17

A freedman is a full member of the tribe.[103] 7.18

The dwellers of paradise are mostly simple folk. 7.19

Women will be in the minority in paradise. 7.20

God grants assistance in accordance with a believer's needs. 7.21

God grants patience in accordance with a believer's tribulations. 7.22

The best rendering of filial duty is continued benevolence to your father's loved ones after his death. 7.23

Satan courses through the veins of men like blood. 7.24

Those who thank people best thank God best. 7.25

Having wealth is a test, losing wealth is a test. 7.26

My community's punishment is levied in this world. 7.27

إنّ الرجل ليُحَرَم الرزق بالذنب يصيبه ٢٨،٧

إنّ من عباد الله من لو أقسم على الله لأبرّه ٢٩،٧

إنّ لله عباداً يعرفون الناس بالتوسّم ٣٠،٧

إنّ لله عباداً خلقهم لحوائج الناس ٣١،٧

إنّ حقّاً على الله أن لا يرفع شيئاً من الدنيا إلّا وضعه ٣٢،٧

إنّ لجواب الكتاب حقّاً كردّ السلام ٣٣،٧

إنّ في المعاريض لمندوحة عن الكذب ٣٤،٧

إنّ أفضل[١] ما أكل الرجل من كسبه وإنّ ولده من كسبه ٣٥،٧

إنّ المسألة لا تحلّ إلّا لفقر مدقع أو غرم مفظع ٣٦،٧

إنّ قليل العمل مع العلم كثير وكثير العمل مع الجهل قليل ٣٧،٧

إنّ العبد ليدرك بحسن الخلق درجة الصائم القائم ٣٨،٧

إنّ لكلّ دين خلقاً وإنّ خلق هذا الدين الحياء ٣٩،٧

إنّ لكلّ شيء شرفاً وإنّ أشرف المجالس ما ٱستقبل به القبلة ٤٠،٧

إنّ لكلّ أمّة فتنة وإنّ فتنة أمّتي المال ٤١،٧

---

١ ك: (أطيب).

A sinner may be denied sustenance. 7.28

God accepts oaths sworn by some of his servants in his name. 7.29

Some of God's servants intuit the essence of people. 7.30

Some of God's servants were created to help the needy. 7.31

God never elevates anything without bringing it down. 7.32

A letter—like a greeting—deserves an answer. 7.33

Ambiguity circumvents lying. 7.34

The best food is bought with your honest earnings or your children's. 7.35

Begging is only permitted in dire poverty or excessive debt. 7.36

A few deeds done with knowledge count for much, many deeds done in ignorance count for little. 7.37

A good character can secure you as high a station as one who prays and fasts. 7.38

Every religion has its own ethic—our religion's primary ethic is modesty. 7.39

Everything has an honorable aspect—in sitting, it is to face Mecca. 7.40

Every community has its test—my community's is wealth. 7.41

إنّ لكلّ ساع غاية وغاية كلّ ساع الموت ٤٢،٧

إنّ لكلّ عابد شِرّة ولكلّ شرّة فترة ٤٣،٧

إنّ لكلّ قول مصداقًا ولكلّ حقّ حقيقة ٤٤،٧

إنّ لكلّ ملك حمًى وإنّ حمى الله محارمه ٤٥،٧

إنّ لكلّ صائم دعوة ٤٦،٧

إنّ لكلّ شيء بابًا وإنّ باب العبادة الصيام ٤٧،٧

إنّ لكلّ شيء معدنًا ومعدن التقوى قلوب العارفين ٤٨،٧

إنّ لكلّ شيء قلبًا وإنّ قلب القرآن يسٓ ٤٩،٧

إنّ لكلّ نبيّ دعوة وإنّي ٱختبأت دعوتي شفاعة لأمّتي يوم القيامة ٥٠،٧

إنّ المؤمن يؤجر في نفقته كلّها إلّا شيئًا جعله في التراب أو البناء ٥١،٧

إنّ الحسد ليأكل الحسنات كما تأكل النار الحطب ٥٢،٧

إنّ أكثر ما يدخل الناس النار الأَجْوَفان الفم والفرج ٥٣،٧

إنّ أكثر ما يدخل الناس الجنّة تقوى الله وحسن الخلق ٥٤،٧

Every traveler has a destination—the final destination is death. 7.42

Every worshipper begins with fervor and fervor always abates.[104] 7.43

Every statement has a touchstone, every truth a reality. 7.44

Every ruler has a fortress—God's fortress is the sum of his prohibitions. 7.45

Every fast means a prayer granted. 7.46

Everything has a door—the door to worship is fasting. 7.47

Everything has a source—the source of piety is the hearts of those who know God. 7.48

Everything has a heart—the heart of the Qur'an is the surah of Yā Sīn.[105] 7.49

Every prophet has one prayer sure to be granted. I have deferred mine—intercession for my community on judgment day. 7.50

A believer is rewarded for all expenditures, except on estates and mansions. 7.51

Envy consumes deeds just as fire consumes kindling. 7.52

Most people are led to the fire by two orifices—their mouths and their genitals. 7.53

Most people are led to the garden by consciousness of God and beauty of character. 7.54

إنّ الدين بدأ غريباً وسيعود الدين غريباً كما بدأ فطوبى للغرباء ٥٥،٧

إنّ الفتنة تجيء فتنسف العباد نسفاً ينجو العالم منها بعلمه ٥٦،٧

إنّ العين لتدخل الرجل القبر وتدخل الجمل القِدر ٥٧،٧

إنّ الذي يجرّ ثوبه خيلاء لا ينظر الله إليه يوم القيامة ٥٨،٧

إنّ الله يحبّ الرفق في الأمر كلّه ٥٩،٧

إنّ الله جميل يحبّ الجمال ٦٠،٧

إنّ الله يحبّ الملحّين في الدعاء ٦١،٧

إنّ الله يحبّ الأبرار الأخفياء الأتقياء ٦٢،٧

إنّ الله يحبّ المؤمن المحترف ٦٣،٧

إنّ الله يحبّ كلّ قلب حزين ٦٤،٧

إنّ الله يحبّ معالي الأمور وأشرافها ويكره سفسافها ٦٥،٧

إنّ الله يحبّ أن تؤتى رخصته كما يحبّ أن تترك معصيته ٦٦،٧

إنّ الله يحبّ البصر النافذ عند مجيء الشهوات والعقل الكامل عند نزول الشبهات ٦٧،٧
ويحبّ السماحة ولو على تمرات ويحبّ الشجاعة ولو على قتل حيّة

إنّ ربّك يحبّ المحامد ٦٨،٧

إنّ الله يحبّ السهل الطلق ٦٩،٧

Religion began as a stranger, and will return a stranger as before—blessed are the strangers![106] 7.55

Seditions appear and crush believers—your only salvation is your learning. 7.56

The evil eye puts people in the grave and camels in the cooking pot. 7.57

On judgment day God will not look at those who swagger in finery. 7.58

God loves gentleness in everything. 7.59

God is beautiful and loves beauty. 7.60

God loves those who beseech him. 7.61

God loves those who are virtuous, humble, and pious. 7.62

God loves the believer who makes an honest living.[107] 7.63

God loves the grieving heart. 7.64

God loves lofty and noble things, and detests paltry and mean ones. 7.65

God loves his concessions to be observed as well as his prohibitions. 7.66

God loves the eye that sees clearly when desire arises, and the mind that thinks lucidly when doubts descend. He loves liberality, even with a few dates, and he loves courage, even when killing a snake. 7.67

Your lord loves praiseworthy traits. 7.68

God loves the cheerful and easygoing. 7.69

إنّ الله يقبل توبة عبده ما لم يُغَرغِر ٧،٧٠

إنّ الله يبغض العِفرِية النِّفرِية الذي لم يُرزأ في جسمه ولا ماله ٧،٧١

إنّ الله كره لكم العبث في الصلاة والرفث في الصيام والضحك عند المقابر ٧،٧٢

إنّ الله ينهاكم عن قيل وقال وإضاعة المال وكثرة السؤال ٧،٧٣

إنّ الله يَغار للمسلم فلْيَغَر ٧،٧٤

إنّ الله لا يرحم من عباده إلّا الرحماء ٧،٧٥

إنّ الله ليدرأ بالصدقة سبعين مِيتة من السوء ٧،٧٦

إنّ الله لينفع العبد بالذنب يذنبه ٧،٧٧

إنّ الله ليؤيّد هذا الدين بالرجل الفاجر ٧،٧٨

إنّ الله ليرضى عن العبد أن يأكل الأُكلة فيحمده عليها أو يشرب الشَّربة فيحمده عليها ٧،٧٩

إنّ الله إذا أنعم على عبد نعمة أحبّ أن تُرى عليه ٧،٨٠

إنّ الله لا يقبض العلم ٱنتزاعًا ينتزعه من الناس ولكن يقبض العلم بقبض العلماء ٧،٨١

إنّ الله يعطي الدنيا على نيّة الآخرة وأبى أن يعطي الآخرة على نيّة الدنيا ٧،٨٢

إنّ الله ليستحيي من العبد أن يرفع إليه يديه فيردّهما خائبتين ٧،٨٣

God will accept your repentance right up to the death rattle. 7.70

God hates the devious and the cunning who avoid adversity thanks to their health and wealth. 7.71

God abhors fidgeting during the prayer, sex during the fast, and laughter at the graveside. 7.72

God forbids tittle-tattle, the squandering of wealth, and habitual solicitation. 7.73

God defends a Muslim's honor jealously, so he should too. 7.74

God only shows mercy to his servants who are merciful. 7.75

Give alms, and God will protect you from seventy brutal forms of death. 7.76

God helps his servant even through the sins he commits. 7.77

God even enlists the dissolute to support our religion. 7.78

God is pleased with those who offer praise after every bite and sip.[108] 7.79

If God bestows a favor on his servant, he loves to have it show. 7.80

God causes knowledge to die not by plucking it from people's hearts, but through the deaths of the learned. 7.81

God gives this world to those who seek the hereafter, but will not give the hereafter to those who seek this world. 7.82

God is ashamed to turn away hands raised to him in appeal. 7.83

إنّ الله جعل لي الأرض مسجدًا وطهورًا ٨٤،٧

إنّ الله زوى لي الأرض فرأيت مشارقها ومغاربها وإنّ ملك أمّتي سيبلغ ما زُوي لي منها ٨٥،٧

إنّ الله تجاوز لأمّتي عمّا حدّثت به أنفسها ما لم تكلّم به أو تعمل به ٨٦،٧

إنّ الله بقسطه وعدله جعل الرَّوح والفرج في اليقين والرضى وجعل الهمّ والحزن في الشكّ والسخط ٨٧،٧

إنّ الله كتب الغَيرة على النساء والجهاد على الرجال فمن صبر منهم[١] ٱحتسابًا كان له مثل أجر شهيد ٨٨،٧

إنّ الله عند لسان كلّ قائل ٨٩،٧

إنّ الله لا يقبل عمل عبد حتّى يرضى قوله ٩٠،٧

إنّ الله إذا أراد بقوم خيرًا ٱبتلاهم ٩١،٧

إنّ أشدّ الناس عذابًا يوم القيامة عالم لم ينفعه الله بعلمه ٩٢،٧

إنّ شرّ الناس عند الله يوم القيامة مَن فَرِقَه الناس ٱتّقاء فحشه ٩٣،٧

إنّ من شرّ الناس عند الله يوم القيامة عبد أذهب آخرته بدنيا غيره ٩٤،٧

إنّ أشقى الأشقياء من ٱجتمع عليه فقر الدنيا وعذاب الآخرة ٩٥،٧

---

١ ت، م: (منهنّ . . . كان له . . .) [كذا].

God gave me the earth as a place of worship and purification. 7.84

God drew together the whole earth so I could glimpse both East and West—truly, my community shall encompass it all. 7.85

God forgives my community its unworthy thoughts, as long as they are not spoken out loud or acted upon. 7.86

God is just and fair. He has made joy and happiness contingent on conviction and acceptance, and grief and sorrow the result of doubt and rejection. 7.87

God has ordained jealousy for women and jihad for men—those who accept God's will and forbear will be rewarded as martyrs.[109] 7.88

God is close by the tongue of every speaker. 7.89

God accepts your deeds only when he is also pleased with your words. 7.90

God visits tribulation on a people he wishes to bless. 7.91

On judgment day, the learned man who has not benefited from his learning will receive the severest punishment. 7.92

On judgment day, the man whose foul mouth is feared will be deemed the most evil. 7.93

On judgment day, the man who has squandered his share of the hereafter on increasing another's share of the world will be deemed the most evil. 7.94

The most wretched of all are those for whom poverty in this world is followed by punishment in the hereafter. 7.95

إنّي أخاف على أمّتي بعدي أعمالاً ثلاثة زلّة عالم وحكم جائر وهوًى متّبع ٩٦،٧

إنّي ممسك بحُجُزكم عن النار وتقاحمون فيها تقاحم الفراش والجنادب ٩٧،٧

إنّا لا نستعمل على عملنا من أراده ٩٨،٧

إنّك لا تدع شيئاً ٱتّقاء الله إلّا أعطاك الله خيراً منه ٩٩،٧

إنّ من موجبات المغفرة إدخال السرور على أخيك المؤمن ١٠٠،٧

إنّ من موجبات المغفرة بذل السلام وحسن الكلام ١٠١،٧

إنّ الدنيا حلوة خضرة وإنّ الله مستخلفكم فيها فناظر كيف تعملون ١٠٢،٧

إنّ من قلب ٱبن آدم بكلّ واد شعبة فمن ٱتّبع قلبه الشعب كلّها لم يبال الله في أيّ واد أهلكه ١٠٣،٧

إنّ هذا الدين متين فأوغل فيه برفق ولا تبغّض إلى نفسك عبادة الله فإنّ المُنبَتّ لا أرضاً قطع ولا ظهراً أبقى ١٠٤،٧

إنّ من السنّة أن يخرج الرجل مع ضيفه إلى باب الدار ١٠٥،٧

إنّ روح القدس نفث في رُوعي أنّ نفسا لن تموت حتّى تستكمل رزقها فٱتّقوا الله وأجملوا في الطلب ١٠٦،٧

I fear three things for my community when I am gone: a scholar's lapse, a tyrant's rule, and a capricious whim. 7.96

You swarm like locusts and rush to the fire like moths. I hold you back by your shirttails. 7.97

We do not appoint those who seek to govern. 7.98

If you give something up for God's sake, he will give you something better. 7.99

Bringing joy to a fellow believer will assuredly win God's mercy. 7.100

Offering the peace-greeting and speaking with kindness will assuredly win God's mercy. 7.101

The world is sweet and green—God has offered it to you and is watching to see what you do. 7.102

Man's heart is inclined to follow many desires[110]—for the heart which follows them all, it is all the same to God which one causes his death. 7.103

Our religion is strong and durable, so press ahead, but gently—do not make worship a burden. A hasty traveler neither reaches his destination nor spares his camel's back. 7.104

Custom dictates that a man accompany his guest to the door. 7.105

The Hallowed Spirit whispered in my heart that no one will die before he has used up his lot, so fear God and be careful in what you seek. 7.106

إنّ ممّا أدرك الناس من كلام النبوّة الأولى إذا لم تستحي فاصنع ما شئت ١٠٧،٧

إنّ في الصلوة لشغلاً ١٠٨،٧

إنّ المصلّي ليقرع باب الملك وإنّه من يُدم قرع الباب يوشك أن يفتح له ١٠٩،٧

إنّ ربّي أمرني أن يكون نطقي ذكرًا وصمتي فكرًا ونظري عبرة ١١٠،٧

إنّما أنا رحمة مُهداة ١١١،٧

إنّما شفاء العِيّ السؤال ١١٢،٧

إنّما يعرف الفضل لأهل الفضل ذوو الفضل ١١٣،٧

إنّما بُعثت لأُتمّم مكارم الأخلاق ١١٤،٧

إنّما أخاف على أمّتي الأئمّة المضلّين ١١٥،٧

إنّما الأعمال بالخواتيم ١١٦،٧

إنّما التصفيح للنساء ١١٧،٧

إنّما بقي من الدنيا بلاء وفتنة ١١٨،٧

إنّما الرضاعة من المجاعة ١١٩،٧

إنّ هذه القلوب تصدأ كما يصدأ الحديد قيل فما جلاؤها قال ذِكر الموت وتلاوة القرآن ١٢٠،٧

Among the first words people heard from the prophet were: If you will not practice modesty, then do as you like. 7.107

Prayer is enough to keep you busy. 7.108

One who prays knocks at a king's door—keep knocking and you may well see the door open. 7.109

My lord commanded that with my words I should invoke him, in my silences I should reflect on him, and through my scrutiny I should learn about him. 7.110

Truly, I am a gift of mercy. 7.111

The cure for ignorance is inquiry. 7.112

The honorable know the honor due the honorable.[111] 7.113

I was sent to perfect noble behavior. 7.114

I fear leaders who will lead my community astray. 7.115

Deeds are judged by outcomes. 7.116

Women should clap.[112] 7.117

Trial and tribulation are all that remain of the world. 7.118

Breastfeeding a hungry baby makes marriage unlawful.[113] 7.119

Hearts can rust, like iron. *He was asked, "How can we burnish them?" and he replied:* By being mindful of death and reciting the Qur'an. 7.120

ألا إنّ عمل الجنّة حَزْن بربوة ١٢١،٧

ألا إنّ عمل النار أو قال الدنيا سهل بسهوة[١] ١٢٢،٧

١ ك: (ألا إنّ عمل أهل النار أو قال أهل الدنيا . . .).

The road to the garden is steep. 7.121

The road to the fire is easy. *Or he said:* The road to worldly things is easy. 7.122

الباب الثامن

ليس الخبر كالمعاينة ١،٨

ليس لفاسق غيبة ٢،٨

ليس لِعِرقِ ظالم حقّ ٣،٨

ليس مِن خُلُق المؤمن الملق ٤،٨

ليس بعد الموت مستعتَب ٥،٨

ليس منّا مَن وسّع الله عليه ثمّ قتّر على عياله ٦،٨

ليس منّا من تشبّه بغيرنا ٧،٨

ليس منّا من لم يتغنّ بالقرآن ٨،٨

ليس منّا من لم يوقّر الكبير ويرحم الصغير ويأمر بالمعروف وينه عن المنكر ٩،٨

ليس بكذّاب من أصلح بين آثنين فقال خيرًا أو نمى خيرًا ١٠،٨

ليس الغنى عن كثرة العرَض إنّما الغنى غنى النفس ١١،٨

Chapter Eight

Hearing is not like seeing. 8.1

Denigrating a debauchee is not slander. 8.2

Farming usurped land earns no rights. 8.3

A believer does not flatter. 8.4

There is no atonement after death. 8.5

If God has given you plenty and you still penny-pinch with your family, you are not one of us. 8.6

If you follow the practices of other faiths, you are not one of us. 8.7

If you do not intone the Qur'an, you are not one of us. 8.8

If you do not respect the elderly, show kindness to the young, command good, and forbid evil, you are not one of us. 8.9

If you reconcile two people, you cannot be reckoned a liar—your words and exaggerations are for the good. 8.10

Worldly goods do not constitute wealth—true wealth is the wealth of the soul. 8.11

ليس الشديد بالصُّرَعة إنّما الشديد الذي يملك نفسه عند الغضب ١٢،٨

ليس شيء أكرم على الله من الدعاء ١٣،٨

ليس شيء أسرع عقوبة من بغي ١٤،٨

ليس شيء خيرًا من ألف مثله إلّا المؤمن ١٥،٨

ليس لك من مالك إلّا ما أكلت فأفنيت أو لبست فأبليت أو تصدّقت فأمضيت ١٦،٨

Throwing people to the ground does not make you strong—true strength belongs to those who can control their anger. 8.12

Nothing is dearer to God than supplication. 8.13

Nothing is punished faster than injustice. 8.14

A single believer is better than a thousand of anything. 8.15

The only possessions that are truly yours are the food you have consumed, the clothes you have worn out, and the alms you have given away. 8.16

الباب التاسع

خير الذكر الخفيّ ١،٩

وخير الرزق ما يكفي ٢،٩

خير العبادة أخفّها ٣،٩

خير المجالس أوسعها ٤،٩

خير دينكم أيسره ٥،٩

خير النكاح أيسره ٦،٩

خير الصدقة ما كان عن ظهر غنى ٧،٩

خير العمل ما نفع ٨،٩

وخير الهدى ما أُتبع ٩،٩

خير ما ألقي في القلب اليقين ١٠،٩

خير الناس أنفعهم للناس ١١،٩

خير الأصحاب عند الله خيرهم لصاحبه ١٢،٩

Chapter Nine

A private invocation is best. 9.1

Adequate sustenance is best. 9.2

The lightest worship is best. 9.3

The most commodious assembly is best. 9.4

The best part of your religion is the most accommodating. 9.5

The most accommodating marriage is best. 9.6

The best alms are those given by the wealthy. 9.7

Beneficial deeds are best. 9.8

Guidance that is followed is best. 9.9

Conviction is the best thing a heart can have. 9.10

The best people are those who benefit others. 9.11

The best companion in God's eyes is the man who helps his fellows best. 9.12

خير الرفقاء أربعة وخير الطلائع أربع مائة وخير الجيوش أربعة آلاف ٩،١٣

خيركم من تعلّم القرآن وعلّمه ٩،١٤

خيركم خيركم لأهله ٩،١٥

خيركم من يُرجى خيره ويؤمَن شرّه ٩،١٦

خير بيوتكم بيت فيه يتيم مكرَّم ٩،١٧

خير المال سكّة مأبورة وفرس مأمورة ٩،١٨

خير مساجد النساء قعر بيوتهنّ ٩،١٩

إنّ من[١] خير ثيابكم البياض ٩،٢٠

وإنّ من خير أكحالكم الإثمِد ٩،٢١

خير شبابكم من تشبّه بكهولكم وشرّ كهولكم من تشبّه بشبابكم ٩،٢٢

خير صفوف الرجال أوّلها وشرّها آخرها وخير صفوف النساء آخرها وشرّها أوّلها ٩،٢٣

اليد العليا خير من اليد السفلى ٩،٢٤

ما قلّ وكفى خير ممّا كثر وألهى ٩،٢٥

الدنيا متاع وخير متاعها المرأة الصالحة ٩،٢٦

---

١ ك: حذفت (من).

Four is the best number for traveling, four hundred the best for a scouting party, and four thousand the best for an army. 9.13

The best of you are those who study and teach the Qur'an. 9.14

The best of you are those who are good to your family. 9.15

The best of you are those whose goodness is assured and from whom no one need fear any evil. 9.16

Homes that shelter orphans are best. 9.17

A row of fecund date-palms and a fertile mare are the best wealth. 9.18

The privacy of the home is the best place for women to pray. 9.19

White garments are best. 9.20

Antimony is the best collyrium.[114] 9.21

Young people who imitate their elders are best, and elders who behave like wanton youths are worst. 9.22

The front row is best for men to pray in, the back row the worst. The back row is best for women, the front the worst. 9.23

The hand that gives is better than the hand that takes.[115] 9.24

Scarce but adequate is better than plentiful but distracting. 9.25

The world is full of delights—the best is a pious woman. 9.26

الوحدة خير من الجليس السوء والجليس الصالح خير من الوحدة ٢٧،٩

وإملاء الخير خير من السكوت والسكوت خير من إملاء الشرّ ٢٨،٩

استتمام المعروف خير من ٱبتدائه ٢٩،٩

عمل قليل في سنّة خير من عمل كثير في بدعة ٣٠،٩

خياركم كلّ مفتَّن توّاب ٣١،٩

خياركم[١] أحسنكم قضاء ٣٢،٩

خيار المؤمنين القانع وشرارهم الطامع ٣٣،٩

خيار أمّتي علماؤها وخيار علمائها حلماؤها ٣٤،٩

خيار أمّتي أحدّاؤها الذين إذا غضبوا رجعوا ٣٥،٩

أفضل الصدقة اللسان ٣٦،٩

أفضل الصدقة إصلاح[٢] ذات البين ٣٧،٩

أفضل الصدقة على ذي الرحم الكاشح ٣٨،٩

أفضل العبادة ٱنتظار الفرَج ٣٩،٩

أفضل عبادة أمّتي قراءة القرآن ٤٠،٩

١ في جميع المخطوطات رواية إضافية: (خيركم). ٢ في جميع المخطوطات رواية إضافية: (صلاح).

Solitude is better than evil company, but virtuous company is better than solitude. 9.27

Good discourse is better than silence, but silence is better than evil discourse. 9.28

Carrying through an act of charity is even better than embarking on it. 9.29

A few exemplary deeds are better than many dubious ones. 9.30

The best of you are sinners who repent. 9.31

The best of you are those who promptly repay debts. 9.32

The best believers are content, the worst greedy. 9.33

The learned are the best in my community, and the levelheaded are the best of the learned. 9.34

The best in my community are those who rein in their anger. 9.35

The greatest charity comes from the tongue.[116] 9.36

The greatest charity is to reconcile the estranged. 9.37

The greatest charity goes to estranged kin. 9.38

The greatest form of worship is to await succor. 9.39

My community's greatest form of worship is to recite the Qur'an. 9.40

أفضل الحسنات تكرمة الجلساء ٩،٤١

أفضل الجهاد كلمة حقّ عند أمير جائر ٩،٤٢

أفضل الفضائل أن تصل من قطعك وتعطي من حرمك وتصفح عمّن ظلمك ٩،٤٣

أفضل العبادة الفقه وأفضل الدين الورع ٩،٤٤

فضل العلم أفضل من العبادة ٩،٤٥

ما من عمل أفضل من إشباع كبد جائع ٩،٤٦

ما تقرّب العبد الى الله بشيء أفضل من سجود خفيّ ٩،٤٧

ما نحل والد ولده أفضل من أدب حسن ٩،٤٨

أحبّ العباد الى الله الأتقياء الأخفياء ٩،٤٩

أحبَّ الله عبداً سمحاً بائعاً ومشترياً وقاضياً ومقتضياً ٩،٥٠

أَحَبُّ البقاع الى الله المساجد ٩،٥١

أحبّ الأعمال الى الله أدومها وإن قلّ ٩،٥٢

إنّ أحبّ الناس الى الله يوم القيامة وأدناهم منه مجلساً إمام عادل ٩،٥٣

الخلق كلّهم عيال الله فأحبّهم إليه أنفعهم لعياله ٩،٥٤

Generosity to people around you is the deed most rewarded. 9.41

A true word to a ruthless ruler is the greatest form of jihad. 9.42

The greastest virtues—to offer friendship to those who cut their ties with you, to give gifts to those who disown you, and to forgive those who wrongs. 9.43

Discernment is the greatest form of worship, scrupulosity the best form of religion. 9.44

The virtues of knowledge are superior to worship. 9.45

There is no deed better than filling a hungry stomach. 9.46

Prostration to God in private is the best way for a worshipper to get close to him. 9.47

Good manners are the best gift parents can give children. 9.48

God's most beloved servants conceal their piety. 9.49

God loves those who show indulgence, be they buyer or seller, payer or collector. 9.50

God's most beloved places are places of worship. 9.51

God's favorite deeds are those performed regularly, even the small ones. 9.52

Just leaders will be God's favorites and closest to his throne on judgment day. 9.53

We are all children of God, and God loves best those who most benefit his children. 9.54

ما صلّت ٱمرأة صلاة أحبّ إلى الله من صلاتها في أشدّ بيتها ظلمة ٥٥،٩

ما من جرعة أحبّ إلى الله من جرعة غيظ كظمها رجل أو جرعة صبر على مصيبة ٥٦،٩

وما من قطرة أحبّ إلى الله من قطرة دمع من خشية الله أو قطرة دم أُهريقت في سبيل الله ٥٧،٩

نعم الشفيع القرآن لصاحبه يوم القيامة ٥٨،٩

نعم الهديّة الكلمة من كلام الحكمة ٥٩،٩

نعم المال النخل الراسخات في الوحل المطعمات في المحل ٦٠،٩

نِعمّا بالمال الصالح للرجل الصالح ٦١،٩

نعم العون على تقوى الله المال ٦٢،٩

نعم الشيء الفأل ٦٣،٩

نعم الإدام الخلّ ٦٤،٩

نعم صَومعة المسلم بيته ٦٥،٩

أصدق الحديث كتاب الله ٦٦،٩

وأوثق العُرى كلمة التقوى ٦٧،٩

وأحسن الهدى هدى الأنبياء ٦٨،٩

وأشرف الموت قتل الشهداء ٦٩،٩

No woman's ritual-prayer is dearer to God than one performed in the most private part of her home. 9.55

Swallow your anger when you are provoked and drink from the cup of forbearance when disaster strikes—this is most beloved of God. 9.56

Tears shed in awe of God, or blood spilled in his service, are most beloved of God. 9.57

How excellently will the Qur'an intercede for its reciters on judgment day! 9.58

What an excellent gift is sound advice! 9.59

What an excellent possession sturdy date-palms are in times of drought! 9.60

How excellent the honest wealth of an honest man! 9.61

How excellent is wealth spent in the service of piety! 9.62

How excellent are good omens! 9.63

How excellent a condiment is vinegar! 9.64

How excellent a cloister is a Muslim's home! 9.65

The book of God is the truest discourse. 9.66

The righteous word is the firmest support. 9.67

The best guidance is given by prophets. 9.68

Martyrdom is the most honorable death. 9.69

أطيب الطيب المسك ٩،٧٠

سيّد إدامكم الملح ٩،٧١

أسرع الدعاء إجابة دعوة غائب لغائب ٩،٧٢

لقلب ٱبن آدم أسرع تقلّباً من القدر إذا ٱستجمعت غلياً ٩،٧٣

حبّذا المتخلّلون من أمّتي ٩،٧٤

Musk is the most fragrant perfume. 9.70

Salt is your principal condiment. 9.71

An absent man's prayer for the absent is quickest to be answered.[117] 9.72

Men change heart more quickly than a pot comes to a boil. 9.73

The truly excellent in my community are those who brush their teeth after meals. 9.74

الباب العاشر

بئس مطيّة الرجل زعموا ١،١٠

شرّ الأمور محدثاتها ٢،١٠

وشرّ العمى عمى القلب ٣،١٠

وشرّ المعذرة حين يحضر الموت ٤،١٠

وشرّ الندامة يوم القيامة ٥،١٠

وشرّ المآكل أكل[١] مال اليتيم ٦،١٠

وشرّ المكاسب كسب الربا ٧،١٠

شرّ ما في الرجل شحّ هالع أو جبن خالع ٨،١٠

أعمى العمى الضلالة بعد الهدى ٩،١٠

ومن أعظم الخطايا اللسان الكذوب ١٠،١٠

ما ملأ آدميّ وعاء شرًّا من بطن ١١،١٠

---

١ ك: حذفت (أكل).

Chapter Ten

"They claim . . ." is the worst horse to ride. 10.1

Heresies are the wickedest things. 10.2

The worst blindness is the heart's. 10.3

The worst excuse is made at the time of death. 10.4

The worst regret is on judgment day. 10.5

An orphan's property is the worst thing to consume. 10.6

The vilest earnings come from usury. 10.7

A man's worst traits is intense avarice or unrestrained cowardice. 10.8

The worst form of blindness is error after guidance. 10.9

The greatest sins come from a lying tongue. 10.10

Humans fill nothing viler than their stomachs. 10.11

الباب الحادي عشر

١،١١ مَثَلُ أهل بيتي مثل سفينة نوح من ركب فيها نجى ومن تخلّف عنها غرق

٢،١١ مثل أصحابي مثل النجوم من ٱقتدى بشيء منها ٱهتدى

٣،١١ إنّ مثل أصحابي في أمّتي كالملح في الطعام لا يصلح الطعام إلّا بالملح

٤،١١ مثل أمّتي مثل المطر لا يُدرى أوّله خير أم آخره

٥،١١ مثل المؤمن مثل النخلة لا تأكل إلّا طيّباً ولا تضع إلّا طيّباً

٦،١١ مثل المؤمن والإيمان كمثل الفرس يجول في آخيّته ثمّ يرجع إلى آخيّته

٧،١١ مثل المؤمن القويّ مثل النخلة ومثل المؤمن الضعيف كخامة الزرع

٨،١١ مثل المؤمن مثل السنبلة تحرّكها الريح فتقوم مرّة وتقع أخرى ومثل الكافر مثل الأَرْزة لا تزال قائمة حتّى تنقعر[1]

٩،١١ مثل المؤمنين في توادّهم وتراحمهم كمثل الجسد إذا ٱشتكى بعضه تداعى سائره بالحمّى والسهر

[1] في جميع مخطوطات مسند الشهاب رواية ثانية: (مثل المؤمن مثل الخامة من الزرع تحرّكها . . .)، وثالثة (ومثل المنافق مثل الأرزة . . .).

Chapter Eleven

My kin are like Noah's Ark—those who climb aboard are saved, those who waver are drowned. 11.1

My companions are like stars—those who follow them will be guided. 11.2

My companions are like salt for the community—food only tastes good with salt. 11.3

My community is like rain—no one knows whether the first or last showers are best. 11.4

A believer is like a honey-bee—what it eats is pure and what it produces is pure. 11.5

A believer and belief are like a horse and its tether—even if it strays, it always returns. 11.6

A strong believer is like a date-palm, a weak believer like a stalk of wheat. 11.7

A believer is like a stalk of wheat constantly buffeted by the wind, now upright, now blown to the ground. A disbeliever is like a pine tree, upright until it comes crashing down. 11.8

In their love and care for each other, believers are like one body: if one part is hurt, the rest is afflicted with fever and insomnia. 11.9

مثل القلب مثل ريشة بأرض تقلّبها الرياح ١٠،١١

مثل القرآن مثل الإبل المعقّلة إن عقلها صاحبها أمسكها وإن تركها ذهبت ١١،١١

مثل المنافق كمثل الشاة العائرة بين الغنمين ١٢،١١

مثل المرأة كالضلع إن أردتَ أن تقيمه كسرته وإن ٱستمتعت به ٱستمتعت به وفيه أَوَد ١٣،١١

مثل الجليس الصالح مثل الداريّ إن لم يُحذك من عطره علقك من ريحه ١٤،١١

ومثل الجليس السَّوء مثل صاحب الكِير إن لم يحرقك من شرار ناره علقك من نتنه ١٥،١١

إنّ مثل الصلاة المكتوبة كالميزان من أوفى ٱستوفى ١٦،١١

ما مثلي ومثل الدنيا إلّا كراكب قال في ظلّ شجرة في يوم حارّ ثم راح وتركها ١٧،١١

ما الدنيا في الآخرة إلّا مثل ما يجعل أحدكم إصبعه السبّابة في اليمّ فلينظر بم ترجع[1] ١٨،١١

---

١ ك، ت: رواية إضافيّة (يرجع).

The heart is like a feather blown about by the wind. 11.10

Think of the Qur'an as a tethered camel—tied up it stays, let loose it runs away. 11.11

The hypocrite is like a ewe running back and forth between two flocks. 11.12

A woman is like a rib—if you try to straighten it, it will break. Be happy with it, for all its crookedness.[118] 11.13

A virtuous companion is like a perfume vendor—even if he gives you no perfume, the fragrance will linger. 11.14

An evil companion is like a blacksmith—even if the fire's sparks don't burn you, the stench will linger. 11.15

Think of the ritual-prayer as a scale—give full measure, receive full measure. 11.16

I am in this world like a traveler who takes a nap in the shade of a tree on a hot day, then continues on his way. 11.17

Compared to the hereafter, this world is like putting your finger in the sea. See how much water you can draw! 11.18

الباب الثاني عشر

إذا أراد الله بعبد خيرًا عسله ١،١٢

إذا أراد الله قبض عبد بأرض جعل له فيها حاجة ٢،١٢

إذا أحبّ الله عبدًا حماه الدنيا كما يظلّ أحدكم يحمي سقيمه الماء ٣،١٢

إذا ٱستشاط السلطان تسلّط الشيطان ٤،١٢

إذا نصح العبد لسيّده وأحسن عبادة ربّه كان له الأجر مرّتين ٥،١٢

إذا تقارب الزمان ٱنتقى الموت خيار أمّتي كما ينتقي أحدكم خيار الرطب من الطبق ٦،١٢

إذا ٱشتكى المؤمن أخلصه ذلك من الذنوب كما يخلص الكير خبث الحديد[1] ٧،١٢

إذا أراد الله تعالى إنفاذ قضائه وقدره سلب ذوي العقول عقولهم حتّى ينفذ فيهم قضاؤه وقدره ٨،١٢

١ ظ، ت، م: رواية إضافية (الخبث من الحديد).

Chapter Twelve

God sweetens the good he wills for his servant.[119] 12.1

If God wishes a servant to die in a distant land, he creates a need for him to go there. 12.2

God protects his servant from worldly things when he loves him, just as you prevent some invalids from drinking water. 12.3

When anger inflames a ruler, Satan takes over. 12.4

A servant who serves his earthly master and worships his heavenly lord receives twice the reward. 12.5

When the end time draws near, death will pick the best in my community just as you pick succulent dates from a bowl. 12.6

A believer's suffering removes his sins just as a blacksmith's fire removes slag from iron. 12.7

When God almighty decrees what is fated, he deprives the intelligent of their intelligence until fate has run its course. 12.8

الباب الثالث عشر

كفى بالسلامة داء ١٫١٣

كفى بالموت واعظًا ٢٫١٣

وكفى باليقين غنًى ٣٫١٣

وكفى بالعبادة شغلًا ٤٫١٣

كفى بالمرء إثمًا أن يُضيع من يقوت ٥٫١٣

كفى بالمرء إثمًا أن يحدّث بكلّ ما سمع ٦٫١٣

كفى بالمرء سعادة أن يوثق به في أمر دينه ودنياه ٧٫١٣

Chapter Thirteen

Well-being is all the illness you need. 13.1

Death is all the counsel you need. 13.2

Conviction is all the wealth you need. 13.3

Worship is all the occupation you need. 13.4

Neglecting to feed your family is sin. 13.5

Repeating everything you hear is sin. 13.6

Being trusted in matters of religion and affairs of the world is felicity. 13.7

الباب الرابع عشر

١٫١٤ رُبَّ مبلَّغ أوعى من سامع

٢٫١٤ وربّ حامل فقه إلى من هو أفقه منه

٣٫١٤ ربّ حامل حكمة إلى من هو لها أوعى منه

٤٫١٤ ألا ربّ نفس طاعمة ناعمة في الدنيا جائعة عارية يوم القيامة ألا ربّ نفس جائعة عارية في الدنيا طاعمة ناعمة يوم القيامة

٥٫١٤ ألا ربّ مكرم لنفسه وهو لها مهين ألا ربّ[١] مهين لنفسه وهو لها مكرم

٦٫١٤ ألا ربّ[٢] شهوة ساعة أورثت حزنًا طويلًا

٧٫١٤ ربّ قائم ليس له من قيامه إلّا السهر وربّ صائم ليس له من صيامه إلّا الجوع والعطش[٣]

٨٫١٤ وربّ طاعم شاكر أعظم أجرًا من صائم صابر

---

١ ك: (يا ربّ). ٢ ك: (يا ربّ). ٣ ظ، ت، م: رواية ثانية (ربّ صائم ليس حظّه من صيامه إلّا الجوع والعطش وربّ قائم ليس حظّه من قيامه إلّا السهر)، وثالثة (ربّ قائم حظّه من قيامه السهر وربّ صائم حظّه من صيامه الجوع والعطش).

Chapter Fourteen

Many remember what they heard about far better than those who actually heard it. 14.1

Many convey their modicum of religious knowledge to those more knowledgeable. 14.2

Many convey their modicum of wisdom to those wiser. 14.3

Hear me! On judgment day, many who live a life of ease in this world will go hungry and naked. Hear me! On judgment day, many who go hungry and naked in this world will be granted a life of ease. 14.4

Hear me! Many who honor themselves abase themselves. Many who abase themselves honor themselves. 14.5

Hear me! Many short-lived pleasures bequeath long-lasting grief. 14.6

Many who pray all night gain only lack of sleep. Many who fast all day gain only hunger and thirst. 14.7

Many who eat and give thanks earn greater reward than many who fast and endure. 14.8

الباب الخامس عشر

لولا أنّ السُؤّال يكذبون ما قُدّس من ردّهم ١٥،١

لو تعلمون ما أعلم لضحكتم قليلاً ولبكيتم كثيرًا ١٥،٢

لو تعلم البهائم من الموت ما يعلم ٱبن آدم ما أكلتم سميناً ١٥،٣

لو نظرتم إلى الأجل ومسيره لأبغضتم الأمل وغروره ١٥،٤

لوكان المؤمن في جحر فأرة لقيّض الله له فيه من يؤذيه ١٥،٥

لوكانت الدنيا تزن عند الله جناح بعوضة ما سقى كافرًا منها شربة ماء ١٥،٦

لو أنّ لٱبن آدم واديين من مال لٱبتغى إليهما ثالثًا[١] ولا يملأ جوف ٱبن آدم إلّا التراب ويتوب الله على من تاب ١٥،٧

لو أنّكم تتوكّلون على الله حقّ توكّله لرزقكم كما يرزق الطير تغدو خِماصاً وتروح بِطاناً ١٥،٨

لو لم تذنبوا لجاء الله بقوم يذنبون فيغفر لهم ويدخلهم الجنّة ١٥،٩

لو لم تذنبوا لخشيتُ عليكم ما هو أشدّ من ذلك العُجب العُجب ١٥،١٠

---

١ في جميع المخطوطات رواية إضافيّة: (لوكان . . . واديان . . . واديا ثالثا).

Chapter Fifteen

If beggars never lied, those who refuse them would never be blessed.[120] 15.1

If you knew what I know, you would laugh little and weep long.[121] 15.2

If cattle knew death as men know it, you would never eat a fat animal.[122] 15.3

If you heeded your life as it ticks away, you would come to despise the deceptions of hope. 15.4

God could send something to hurt a believer even if he hid in a burrow. 15.5

If God valued the world even a smidgen—the weight of a gnat's wing—he would not allow disbelievers a single sip of water from it. 15.6

If a person owns two valleys brimful with wealth, he will still seek a third—man's greed is sated only in death.[123] Still, God forgives the repentant. 15.7

If you placed complete trust in God, he would sustain you as he sustains the birds—in the morning their stomachs are empty, by evening their stomachs are full. 15.8

If you never sin, God will create a people who do, then forgive them and grant them paradise. 15.9

Even if you never sin, I fear something much worse for you. Vanity! Vanity! 15.10

الباب السادس عشر

يتضمّن كلمات رويت عن رسول الله صلّى الله عليه وآله عن ربّه تعالى ذكره وجلّت قدرته

يقول الله تعالى

أنا عند ظنّ عبدي بي وأنا مع عبدي إذا ذكرني ١،١٦

وجبت محبّتي للمتحابّين فيّ والمتجالسين فيّ والمتباذلين فيّ والمتزاورين فيّ ٢،١٦

لا إله إلّا الله حصني فمن دخله أمن عذابي ٣،١٦

اشتدّ غضبي على من ظلم من لا يجد ناصرًا غيري ٤،١٦

يا دنيا مُرّي على أوليائي لا تَحَلَوِلي لهم فَتَفْتِنيهم ٥،١٦

يا دنيا ٱخدمي من خدمني وأتعبي يا دنيا من خدمك ٦،١٦

من أهان لي وليًّا فقد بارزني بالمحاربة ٧،١٦

Chapter Sixteen

Sayings of the Lord Reported by the Messenger of God

God has said:[124]

I am as my servant thinks of me, and I am with him whenever he calls. 16.1

I pledge my love to those who love each other for my sake, who sit together for my sake, who use their wealth for my sake, and who visit each other for my sake. 16.2

"There is no god but God" is my citadel—those who enter it are safe from my punishment. 16.3

Intense is my anger against all who oppress those whose only help comes from me. 16.4

Make your taste bitter, world, for all those who love me—do not tempt them with your sweetness. 16.5

Serve those who serve me, world, and weary those who serve you. 16.6

Anyone who demeans those who love me challenges me to battle. 16.7

وما ردّدت في شيء أنا فاعله ما ردّدت في قبض نفس عبدي المؤمن يكره الموت وأكره مساءته ولا بدّ له منه ٨،١٦

ما تقرّب إليّ عبدي المؤمن بمثل الزهد في الدنيا ولا تعبّد لي بمثل أداء ما ٱفترضته عليه ٩،١٦

يا موسى إنّه لم يتصنّع لي بمثل الزهد في الدنيا ولم يتقرّب إليّ المتقرّبون بمثل الورع عمّا حرّمت عليهم ولم يتعبّد إليّ المتعبّدون بمثل البكاء من خيفتي ١٠،١٦

هذا دين ٱرتضيته لنفسي ولن يصلحه إلّا السخاء وحسن الخلق فأكرموه بهما ما صحبتموه ١١،١٦

إذا وجّهت إلى عبد من عبيدي مصيبة في بدنه أو ماله أو ولده ثم ٱستقبل ذلك بصبر جميل ٱستحييت منه يوم القيامة أن أنصب له ميزانًا أو أنشر له ديوانًا[١] ١٢،١٦

الكبرياء ردائي والعظمة إزاري فمن نازعني واحدًا منهما ألقيته في النار ١٣،١٦

١ ظ: تضيف هنا حديثا (إذا شغل عبدي ذكري عن مسألتي أعطيته أفضل ما أعطي السائلين) مع إسناده.

I waver most when taking the life of a believer who hates death. I hate to hurt him, but there is no other way. 16.8

Nothing draws my servant closer than renouncing the world. No form of worship is worthier than the mandatory rites. 16.9

None adorn themselves more beautifully than those who renounce the world. None draw closer than those who refrain from what I have forbidden. None worship more fully than by weeping in awe of me.[125] 16.10

This is the religion I myself have chosen—only generosity and rectitude will do for it. Honor it by practicing them. 16.11

When I afflict my servant's health, wealth, or children, and he accepts this with exemplary fortitude, I will be too embarrassed to weigh his deeds or divulge his ledger on judgment day. 16.12

Grandeur is my robe, majesty my mantle—I shall hurl in the fire those who challenge me for either. 16.13

الباب السابع عشر

هذا باب الدعاء الذي يُختَم به الكتاب

١٠١٧ اللّٰهمّ إنّي أعوذ بك من علم لا ينفع وقلب لا يخشع ودعاء لا يُسْمَع ونفس لا تشبع أعوذ بك من شرّ هؤلاء الأربع

٢٠١٧ اللّٰهمّ إنّي أعوذ بك أن أَضلّ أو أُضلّ أو أَذلّ أو أُذلّ أو أَظلم أو أُظلم أو أَجهل أو يُجهل عليّ

٣٠١٧ اللّٰهمّ إنّي أسألك تعجيل عافيتك وصبرًا على بليّتك وخروجًا من الدنيا إلى رحمتك

٤٠١٧ اللّٰهمّ خِرْ لي وٱختر لي

٥٠١٧ اللّٰهمّ حسّنتَ خَلقي فحسّن خُلُقي[1]

٦٠١٧ اللّٰهمّ إنّك عفوّ تحبّ العفو فٱعف عنّي

٧٠١٧ اللّٰهمّ ٱغفر لي ما أخطأتُ وما تعمّدت وما أسررت وما أعلنت وما جهلت وما تعمّدت[2]

٨٠١٧ اللّٰهمّ آت نفسي تقواها وزكّها أنت خير من زكّاها وأنت وليّها ومولاها

---

١ في جميع المخطوطات رواية إضافيّة: (. . . أحسنت . . . فأحسن . . .). ٢ هكذا في جميع المخطوطات (تعمّدت) مرّتين في الحديث.

Chapter Seventeen

The Final Chapter Containing the Prophet's Supplications

God, I seek refuge with you from knowledge without benefit, from a heart without humility, from a prayer unheard, and from an appetite unsated. I seek refuge with you from the evil of all four. 17.1

God, I seek refuge with you from misleading or being misled, from demeaning or being demeaned, from tormenting or being tormented, from wronging or being wronged. 17.2

God, grant me a speedy cure, fortitude to bear your trials, and passage from this world into your mercy. 17.3

God, choose and single out what is good for me. 17.4

God, you made me beautiful—make my character beautiful too. 17.5

God, you are forgiving and love forgiving—forgive me my sins. 17.6

God, forgive my sins—be they mistaken or deliberate, hidden or public, by omission or commission. 17.7

God, make my soul mindful of you and cleanse it of sin—you cleanse it best, since you are its master and benefactor.[126] 17.8

اللّٰهمّ إنّي أعوذ بك من شرورهم وأدرأ بك في نحورهم ٩،١٧

بك أحاول وبك أقاتل وبك أصول ١٠،١٧

اللّٰهمّ واقية كواقية الوليد ١١،١٧

اللّٰهمّ أذقت أوّل قريش نكالًا فأذق آخرهم نوالًا ١٢،١٧

اللّٰهمّ بارك لأمّتي في بكورها ١٣،١٧

إليك ٱنتهت الأماني يا صاحب العافية ١٤،١٧

ربِّ تقبّل توبتي وٱغسل حوبتي وأجب دعوتي ١٥،١٧

اللّٰهمّ إنّي أسألك عيشة سويّة وميتة نقيّة[١] ومردًّا غير مخز ولا فاضح ١٦،١٧

---

١ ك: (تقيّة).

God, I seek your protection against my enemies' machinations, and your defense against their attacks. 17.9

Through you I strive, through you I fight, through you I attack. 17.10

God, grant me the protection you grant the newborn! 17.11

God, you made the first of the Quraysh taste your punishment, now let the last of them taste your favor.[127] 17.12

God, bless my community when they venture out at first light. 17.13

To you, bestower of well-being, I deliver all my hopes. 17.14

Lord, accept my repentance, wash away my offense, and answer my prayer. 17.15

God, I ask you for a tranquil life, a pure death, and a return to you free from disgrace and dishonor. 17.16

تمّ كتاب الشهاب

والحمد لله وحده

وصلاته على سيّدنا محمّد نبيّه الكريم وآله وسلامه

This completes *Light in the Heavens.*

I offer praise to the one God.

I ask for his peace and blessings
upon our master Muḥammad, his honored prophet,
and upon Muḥammad's progeny.

Notes

1 Q Baqarah 2:119, Saba' 34:28, Fāṭir 35:24, Fuṣṣilat 41:4.

2 Q Aḥzāb 33:46. In Qur'anic usage, *sirāj*, lit. "lamp," is most often metaphorically used for "sun"; see Q Furqān 25:61, Nūḥ 71:16.

3 Q Aḥzāb 33:33.

4 Q Najm 53:3.

5 Q Naml 27:59.

6 Rather than 1,200 sayings, al-Quḍāʿī's collection contains 1,200 clauses. Though none of the manuscripts use numbering, the *Musnad al-Shihāb* editors do so (al-Salafī: 911 sayings, 1,499 reports; al-Maḥallāwī: sayings not numbered, 1,383 reports). I disregard the 1,200 count, as it has no substantive bearing on the compilation.

7 Al-Quḍāʿī, *Musnad al-Shihāb*, ed. al-Silafī, Beirut, 1985; ed. al-Maḥallawī, Beirut, 2011.

8 *Ḥasab* can mean both "virtue" and "lineage" (in the sense that good lineage is considered a virtue). S 1:96, R 73, Y 7, D 40, M 4n1.

9 Lit. "Half of aging is worrying."

10 Lit. "[Having] fewer children is one of two modes of affluence."

11 Two explanations are common: (1) that this has the same meaning as another hadith, "Do not have your child suckled by a woman who is foolish or has weak eyesight, for milk transmits these deficiencies"; or (2) that if the wet nurse has a bad character, her milk will pass it on to the child she suckles, even if the parents are good, moral people. R 84.

12 "Book" may refer to: (1) the Qur'an, or (2) any book of knowledge. The word *kitāb* can also mean "letter," and in this interpretation, *khatm* (translated here as "full") would mean "seal." The hadith would then be translated as "Give your letter due honor by sealing it." R 86.

13 Lit. "A wise word is the sage's lost camel." I.e., it belongs to him, and he should seize it wherever he finds it.

14 Lit. "the age of ignorance" (Ar. *jāhiliyyah*), a term denoting the pre-Islamic period in which most tribal inhabitants of the Arabian Peninsula were pagan. Ignorance here is usually interpreted as ignorance of the one true God.

15 I.e., the suffering caused by fever serves as atonement for believers' sins. R 99.

16 This hadith has been interpreted to mean either (1) that if a poor man gives away what little he has and so cannot feed himself and his family, he is wrong to do so, and will not be rewarded for his charity; or (2) that an alms-levy collector should not commandeer the choicest part of a taxpayer's property, as this could lead to the taxpayer not paying any taxes the following year. R 122; M 19–20n4; Ibn Manẓūr, *Lisān al-ʿarab*, s.v. *ʿ-D-Y*.

17 Lit. "Oppression [will manifest as] darkness on judgment day."

18 Lit. "Every burning liver reaps a rich reward." Medieval Muslims—like the ancient Greeks—deemed the liver to be the seat of emotions.

19 I.e., those who are killed fighting for truth will be rewarded with paradise.

20 I.e., between the call (*adhān*) and summons (*iqāmah*) to the ritual-prayer is a propitious time for supplication.

21 Lit. "A believer consumes with a single gut . . ."

22 Muslims can fast easily in winter because of shorter days, and pray longer at night because of longer nights. Y 35–36.

23 Lit. "Wisdom is the sage's lost camel." I.e., it belongs to him, and he should seize it wherever he finds it.

24 Three explanations are provided by the commentators: (1) that it underscores the Yemenis' speedy entry into the fold of Islam; (2) that the people of Medina were for the most part originally from Yemen; or (3) that the prophet actually meant Mecca and Medina, since the lands of Yemen include Tihamah and Hijaz, in which Mecca and Medina are located, or because the prophet spoke this hadith when he was in Tabuk, and Mecca and Medina lie between Tabuk and Yemen. Y 40, S 1:371, R 148–49, M 30n2.

25 Although the generic male term "all Muslims" includes both men and women, other compilers cite this hadith with a more explicit dual gender: "It is every Muslim man and woman's obligatory duty to seek knowledge" (طلب العلم فريضة على كلّ مسلم ومسلمة). See al-Qāḍī al-Nuʿmān, *Daʿāʾim al-Islām*, 1:83.

26 The term "emigration" refers to those who migrated with Muḥammad from Mecca to Medina. This hadith connects migration and rejection by punning: "emigrant" (*muhājir*) and "reject" (*hajara*) both derive from the same root *H-J-R*.

27 There are two dominant interpretations: The first is that one is resurrected in the hereafter with the person one followed in life, explained by the context, which is that the prophet asked a Bedouin, "What have you prepared for the hour?" and the man replied that he prayed little but loved those who prayed. Muḥammad then said, "You are with those you love." The second is that a man's heart is always with the person he loves. Y 44, R 160–61, S 375, M 34n3.

28 Lit. "A man's Islam . . ."—*islām* means commitment [to God's will].

29 I.e., people's value stems from their inner morality; an alternative interpretation is that the value of what is inside them is known only by deep probing. R 163, S 1:382.

30 I.e., most people are ignorant and base, and it is hard to find a single righteous individual among any group; an alternative interpretation is that all are equal in the eyes of the law. R 163, S 1:383.

31 Alternatively, "Every man suffices for himself." Y 46.

32 A reference to the importance of horses for the defense of the community. Y 48–49, S 1:392, M 40n4.

33 A prayer-leader is important because the validity of the congregation's ritual-prayer depends on his not committing errors. Y 52, M 43n2.

34 Lit. "will have the longest necks." According to al-Qāḍī al-Nuʿmān (*Daʿāʾim al-Islām*, 1:144), muezzins will have long necks on judgment day because they will gaze at God's mercy, in contrast to "criminals," who will be «hanging their heads before their lord» (Q Sajdah 32:12).

35 The Allies (*anṣār*) are the people of Yathrib/Medina who supported Muḥammad in the early years of Islam, when he migrated there from Mecca.

36 Muḥammad reportedly spoke these words to console himself for his daughter Ruqayyah's death in 2/624. S 1:406–7, Y 55, M 46n3.

37 I.e., the average lifespan. R 187–88.

38 This hadith means that when one party demands that the other take an oath in lieu of witness testimony, the oath will be construed in regard to the matter in dispute: in Islamic law, if a case cannot be resolved by the oral testimony of an eyewitness, the defendant is required to swear an oath to support his claim. The rule expressed in this hadith is designed to prevent the oath-taker from using ambiguous language to mislead the tribunal. I thank Joseph Lowry for his help in annotating this line.

39 *[Ahl] al-dhimmah*, lit. "protected people" and translated here as "subjects," refers in the classical period primarily to Jews and Christians.

40 Lit. "Dirt is children's springtime."

41 "What they have taken" is interpreted as meaning either (1) things borrowed or accepted in trust, or (2) things seized unlawfully. Y 61, S 1:418, R 197–98, M 52n2.

42 Lit. "The child belongs to the marital bed; the fornicator gets stones." The first part means that even if there is suspicion regarding a wife's fidelity, the children she bears are legitimate, and the man she may have fornicated with has no claims over the child. The second part is a reference to the fact that fornicators should be punished by stoning. The context for the hadith is that a man said, "O messenger of God, this is my son; I fornicated with his mother during the age of ignorance [i.e., before Islam]," and

Muḥammad replied: "No claims can be made regarding the age of ignorance. Married couples can claim their offspring, adulterers can claim only their punishment—stones." R 198, Y 61, S 1:419–20, M 52–53n3.

43 The commentators all agree that this is because it is more practical and customary for the Bedouin than city dwellers to shelter guests. R 199, S 1:420, M 53n1.

44 I.e., do not assume someone has means just because he looks or behaves like he does. R 200.

45 Three explanations are given: (1) that looking at greenery and at a beautiful woman who is legal to you gives you pleasure and thus increases your eyes' sparkle, (2) that doing so increases your awe of the creator and brings a sparkle to your inner eye, and (3) that looking at greenery heals ophthalmia, or inflammation of the eye. R 201, S 1:423, M 53–54n5.

46 Speaking during the ritual-prayer invalidates it. This hadith refers either to the method of response if someone is addressed when they are performing the ritual-prayer, or to the method for alerting the prayer-leader to an error.

47 Lit. "one of twenty-six parts of prophethood."

48 Commentators have explained the first part of the hadith as referring to either (1) someone who pretends to asceticism, worship, and restraint from dubious actions when his heart does not truly possess those qualities; or (2) a co-wife who, in order to cause distress, falsely boasts to another co-wife that their husband loves and cherishes her more (this saying being the prophet's response to such a co-wife who came to him to confess). The two false garments are explained as gross lies and false display, or garments worn one on top of another by a person bearing false witness who comes to the judge hoping his imposing demeanor will pressure the judge into accepting his testimony, or the two sleeves (one on top and one extra) attached to a person's garment on each side to give the impression that he is wearing two full garments, suggesting wealth. S 1:437; R 209; Y 67; M 58n3; al-Nawawī, *Sharḥ Ṣaḥīḥ Muslim*, 14:110; Ibn Ḥajar, *Fatḥ al-bārī*, 9:318.

49 I.e., the deliberate or unwitting spreading of falsehoods by "tellers of tales," popular preachers who embellish stories from the Qur'an, incurs God's wrath. The audiences are exonerated, since they listen with pure hearts and hope to learn. R 211, S 1:440, M 58–59n4.

50 The hadith continues: "The judge who will go to paradise knows the truth and judges by it. As for the two who will burn in hellfire—one knows the truth yet contravenes it in his judgment, the other passes judgment in ignorance." R 213–14.

51 Alternatively, "Anyone who [tyrannizes others] using the strength of his multitude of slaves, God brings to his knees." R 228, S 1:465.

52 Trimming the mustache was encouraged by Muḥammad. S 1:466.

53 Because this was not the practice of the prophet.

54 Lit. ". . . as the nest of a sandgrouse."

55 ʿAbd al-Muṭṭalib was Muḥammad's paternal grandfather.

56 A reference to the pre-Islamic practice of female infanticide condemned in the Qur'an. Q Takwīr 81:8–9: «When on judgment day the buried girl is asked: For what crime was she killed?» ﴿وَإِذَا ٱلْمَوْءُۥدَةُ سُئِلَتْ بِأَىِّ ذَنۢبٍ قُتِلَتْ﴾.

57 Reference to Q ʿAnkabūt 29:45: «Perform the daily prayer, for prayer restrains from indecency and misdeeds» ﴿وَأَقِمِ ٱلصَّلَاةَ إِنَّ ٱلصَّلَاةَ تَنْهَىٰ عَنِ ٱلْفَحْشَآءِ وَٱلْمُنكَرِ﴾.

58 The East Wind, Ṣabā is a rain-bearing wind that blows toward the Kaaba; it is apparently so-called because it yearns (*taṣbū*) for the Kaaba. ʿĀd is the name of an ancient Arabian tribe said to have been destroyed by God with Dabūr, a fierce west wind said to blow away from—or have its back (*dubur*) to—the Kaaba. Muḥammad is said to have spoken these words after the Battle of the Confederates in 5/627, or the Battle of Badr in 2/624. S 1:530–31, R 275–76.

59 See Q Ṭalāq 65:2–3: «For anyone who is conscious of God, he grants a way out, and provides for him from an unexpected source [or «in a manner beyond expectation»]; and anyone who places his trust in God, he suffices» ﴿. . . وَمَن يَتَّقِ ٱللَّهَ يَجْعَل لَّهُۥ مَخْرَجًا وَيَرْزُقْهُ مِنْ حَيْثُ لَا يَحْتَسِبُ وَمَن يَتَوَكَّلْ عَلَى ٱللَّهِ فَهُوَ حَسْبُهُۥ . . .﴾. S 1:535, R 280, M 100n3.

60 An indication of the first part's ambiguity is the numerous explanations offered by commentators: (1) poverty pushes a person to do all kinds of things to obtain sustenance, many of which might be forbidden in Islam; (2) since poverty and wealth are decreed by God, a lack of acceptance of one's indigent state can be construed as a challenge to God; (3) "poverty" means "poverty of the heart," i.e., a lack of contentment; (4) "poverty" means "paucity of good deeds"; or (5) people look down on a poor man as they look down on a disbeliever. Cf. S 1:535–36, R 280–81, M 100–101n4.

61 For the second part, the following explanations are offered: (1) by his envy, the envier is challenging, or at the very least refusing to accept, God's decreeing of wealth for the person he envies; (2) the point is to censure envy, not to say that it can actually change God's decree; (3) envy is similar to "the eye" in terms of its evil effect; or (4) the envier tries to destroy the person he envies, and thus tries to overthrow God's decree. S 1:536–37, R 281, M 100–101n4.

62 The commentaries prefix a phrase to the hadith, which renders it "I wonder at a believer's displeasure with God's providence" (عجباً للمؤمن لا يرضى بقضاء الله . . .). R 283–84, S 1:541, M 103n1.

63 Cf. New Testament, Matthew 7:31.

64 ʿAmr ibn Umayyah asked Muḥammad, "O Messenger of God, shall I tie up my camel mare [to ensure she does not wander away] and have faith in God, or not tie her up and have trust?" He said: "Tie her up and trust in God." N 1:368.

65 An injunction against marrying an immoral woman, as her vices are likely to influence the character of her offspring. R 303, S 2:559–60, M 110–11n3.

66 The text addresses a companion of the prophet nicknamed Abū Hirr, who is more commonly known as Abu Hurayrah (d. 58/678).

67 I.e., help your brother by coming to his aid when he is being oppressed, and by stopping him from oppressing. It is worded in language deliberately similar to a slogan common in pre-Islamic times exhorting people to side with their tribal brethren whether they were in the right or in the wrong. R 306.

68 The command to emigrate is interpreted as an exhortation (1) to Muslims living in the time of the prophet to emigrate to his city, Medina, and (2) to Muslims living in any period to travel afar to seek knowledge and livelihood. R 312, M 115n1.

69 Lit. "Be ever mindful of the destroyer of pleasures." The "destroyer of pleasures" is explained as death. R 317.

70 This is an exhortation against overdoing things, even good things, or an injunction to console oneself in hard times by remembering the coming joys of the hereafter. S 2:579–80, R 318, M 118n2.

71 In the sense that wearing dignified garments encourages dignity and self-control. S 1:318, R 317, M 118n3.

72 Muḥammad said: "For each person among you, God has decreed a seat in hellfire or paradise." So he was asked, "Messenger of God, does that mean our fate is written and we should stop performing good deeds?" and he responded (this response is the *Shihāb* hadith), "Act, for the actions a person has been created to perform come naturally: The deeds of the blissful come naturally to them. The deeds of the wretched come naturally to them." Then he recited, «As for one who gives to others, fears God, and believes in the truth of what is right, I shall pave his way to ease. But as for one who is stingy and unheeding, and denies what is right, I shall pave his way to hardship» (Q Layl 92:5–10). Al-Bukhārī, *Al-Jāmiʿ al-ṣaḥīḥ*, 4:1891; Muslim, *Ṣaḥīḥ*, 4:2040.

73 A reference to the pre-dawn meal eaten during Ramadan.

74 An exhortation to charity, no matter how small. R 320, S 2:582–83, M 119n3.

75 An injunction against soliciting even for paltry things, such as a toothbrush (lit. a small stick of wood with a softened tip used for brushing teeth), or alternatively, for discarded mouth-rinsing water. S 2:569, R 321.

76 An injunction against women displaying themselves in fine clothes and jewels, presumably to unrelated males. R 321–22, S 2:583, M 120n2.

77 An echo of the Qur'anic verse «God extracts the hidden things from the skies and the earth» ﴿ ٱلَّذِي يُخْرِجُ ٱلْخَبْءَ فِي ٱلسَّمَٰوَٰتِ وَٱلْأَرْضِ ﴾ (Q Naml 27:25). The reference is to agriculture and/or mining, or to distant travels. Ibn Manẓūr, *Lisān al-ʿarab*, s.v. *KH-B-ʾ*; Lane, *Lexicon*, s.v. *KH-B-ʾ*; R 325; S 2:585–86; M 121–22n4.

78 This means either (1) value food and do not waste, or (2) be precise and honest in buying and selling commodities, especially food items like grain and dates. R 325–26, S 2:588, M 122n2.

79 One interpretation is that the hadith is an exhortation to amity and brotherhood, specifically in the context of washing hands after eating: the person pouring the water should go to person after person until the basin fills up, and only then should he empty it out. This interpretation is supported by the preceding line of the hadith report, which says: "Do not take away the basin until it fills up." Another interpretation is that the hadith is an exhortation to perform the ablution in a complete manner. N 1:408, R 328, S 2:589.

80 An exhortation to perform the dawn prayer in the latter part of the time slot designated for it. S 2:590, R 328–29.

81 Four interpretations are offered by the commentators: (1) a reference to the *tayammum*, an ablution performed with earth when water is unavailable; (2) an exhortation to perform the prostration (*sujūd*) in the ritual-prayer directly on the earth without using a prayer mat as an expression of humility; (3) an assertion that people will be buried in the earth; or (4) "the earth offers you compassion," meaning that "she is your compassionate mother." R 329; M 123n4; Ibn Manẓūr, *Lisān al-ʿarab*, s.vv. *M-S-Ḥ* and *B-R-R*.

82 Interpreted as an injunction to city dwellers against taking unfair advantage of naive Bedouins in buying and selling goods. R 320–30, M 123–24n4.

83 The word translated as "criminal act" here is *ḥadd* (pl. *ḥudūd*)—a penalty prescribed by Islamic law for murder, theft, adultery, alcohol consumption, and bearing false witness.

84 Q Sharḥ 94:5–6.

85 The text addresses a companion of the prophet named Bilāl, exhorting him to spend on himself and his family and to trust in God to provide. R 347.

86 "May your hands be filled with earth" (تربت يداك) is interpreted as a prayer for one's hands to be filled with good things, and is, as such, an apotropaic idiom—like "May no land offer you shelter!" (لا أرض لك)—so worded to ward off the evil eye. Note that the preceding line in fuller versions of the hadith reads: "Women are wed for their beauty, wealth, and lineage" (تُنكح المرأة لِمِيسمها ولمالها ولحسبها). Ibn Manẓūr, *Lisān al-ʿarab*, s.v. *T-R-B*; R 349–50; M 135n1.

87 The commentators differ in their explanations: The Sunni al-Sijilmāsī says the command to kill a second claimant is not to be taken literally, but rather it means to "kill his fame" and to subdue him by not supporting him (S 2:622). The Shi'i al-Rāwandī explains it in the context of the succession to Muḥammad as the community's obligation to fight to support the rightful incumbent and Muḥammad's appointed successor, 'Alī (R 350).

88 The translation may also be rendered "God never empowers the ignorant or demeans the intelligent," for the hadith's two key terms (often used as a pair) are each bivalent: *jahl*=ignorance/harshness, *ḥilm*=intelligence/forbearance. Lane, *Lexicon*, s.vv. *J-H-L* and *Ḥ-L-M*.

89 Lit. "from the same snake pit twice."

90 *Birr* (translated here as "virtue") can also refer more particularly to filial piety.

91 Alternatively, this is explained as an exhortation to Muslims to perform the hajj pilgrimage. R 376; Lane, *Lexicon*, s.v. *Ṣ-R-R*.

92 A reference to Muḥammad's conquest of Mecca in 8/629; the injunction is against emigration to Medina after the conquest of Mecca and the subsequent spread of Islam in the Arabian Peninsula.

93 The commentators explain this hadith to mean that (1) after the conquest, no enemy will ever challenge the Muslims over Mecca, or that (2) no violence should rend Mecca's sanctity, or that (3) no one would claim bloodwit for the Jewish woman killed for satirizing Muḥammad. R 378, S 2:646.

94 Jurists debate whether this is a blanket injunction against women holding positions of religious, political, juridical, and military leadership, or whether it is specific to the historical context of the prophet learning of a princess succeeding to the Sassanian throne. R 379, S 1:396.

95 *Yu'dhirū* (or *ya'dhirū*), more commonly denoting "to excuse," is interpreted here as "committing many crimes." R 385; S 2:652; M 155n2; Ibn Manẓūr, *Lisān al-'arab*, s.v. *'-DH-R*; Lane, *Lexicon*, s.v. *'-DH-R*.

96 Commentators have offered several interpretations for this cryptic hadith: (1) do not use the services of someone who is not your beneficiary; (2) do not trust someone you have not tested; (3) do not take what does not belong to you; (4) do not meddle with the property of someone you have no jurisdiction over; or (5) do not oppress a believer, no matter how poor, for God, not you, gives him food and clothing. R 396, S 2:664–65, M 160–61n4.

97 Muḥammad himself is said to have explained, "As a man finishes loading up his belongings on his camel, his drinking cup often has some water left in it, so he drinks it up and casually tosses the cup on top of his equipage. . . . Place me at the beginning of your

discourse, in the middle, and at the end." N 2:89; R 401; S 2:668–69; M 164–65n4; Lane, *Lexicon*, s.v. *Q-D-Ḥ*.

98 Lit. "Beware of green plants . . ." Muḥammad was asked, "O Messenger of God, what is meant by plants growing on a dung heap?" And he replied, "A beautiful woman who comes from a foul source," i.e., whose lineage is suspect. R 405, S 1:231–32, M 167n4, N 2:96.

99 Another possible interpretation is "Words are children," i.e., words can be attributed to their speaker in the same way that children are attributed to parents. R 410, S 1:233 and 2:687, M 168n1.

100 This is explained as meaning that either (1) seeking knowledge can lead to ignorance when a scholar mixes what he knows with guesswork, or (2) certain kinds of knowledge—such as philosophy, astrology, "books of the ancients," and music—are detrimental (the permissibility of studying these subjects was often a point of debate among Muslims). R 410, S 2:687–88, M 168n1.

101 The context is that an old woman often used to visit Muḥammad, who treated her with special kindness. When his wife ʿĀʾishah expressed surprise, he responded that she often used to visit his late wife Khadījāh. N 2:102.

102 "Righteous" here translates *ḥanīfiyyah*, related to the Qurʾanic *ḥanīf*, used of the prophet Abraham and by extension for the God-fearing. E.g., Q Baqarah 2:135.

103 Freedmen (*mawālī*, sing. *mawlā*) are former slaves; upon manumission they retained affiliation to their master's tribe.

104 An exhortation to moderation in all things, even worship. R 421, S 2:712, M 176n4.

105 Yā Sīn is the name of the thirty-sixth surah of the Qurʾan. In longer versions, the hadith continues: "By reciting it, he is credited with reciting the entire Qurʾan ten times over" (كتب له بقراءتها قراءة القرآن عشر مرارٍ). N 2:130.

106 The commentators explain that Islam began with few supporters, and at the end of time—after centuries of strength—it will again have few supporters. R 424, S 2:715–16, M 179n3.

107 Alternatively readable as ". . . those who work with their hands."

108 Alternatively, "after every meal and draught."

109 The commentators interpret the first part of the hadith as exhorting co-wives to practice fortitude in the face of jealousy. R 435.

110 Lit. "inclines into every valley."

111 The word *faḍl*, translated here as "honor," also means "generosity."

112 Cf. earlier hadith §1.226.

113 Lit. "suckling is consequent upon hunger." The commentators explain that suckling by a foster mother interdicts the child's subsequent marriage as an adult to the woman who suckled (and to certain of her relatives), when the suckling was to satisfy the child's hunger. If the suckling was occasional, no interdiction applies. R 446; M 183n4; Lane, *Lexicon*, s.v. *J-W-ʿ*.

114 Antimony is a lustrous gray metalloid whose compounds have been used as cosmetics since ancient times. The Arabs used antimony as liner or salve for the eyes for cosmetic effect and for medicinal benefit.

115 Lit. "The hand on top is better than the hand below."

116 In the *Musnad*'s hadith report, Muḥammad was then asked, "What is the tongue's charity?" and he replied, "Intercession—by which you free a captive, prevent blood from being spilled, draw charity and generous gifts to your brother, and ward off his difficulties." S 2:778, N 2:243.

117 Since the person one is praying for is absent, such a prayer is from the heart and far removed from hypocrisy. M 211n4.

118 The commentators say the hadith is (1) an exhortation to men not to argue with women, or (2) an assertion that women are intrinsically flawed. R 492, S 2:812, M 217n4.

119 Lit. "he infuses him with honey." Two explanations are given: (1) that if God wishes something good for his servant, he makes people think well of him in life or after death, or (2) that he guides him to good deeds before he dies. R 499, S 2:814, M 218n3.

120 This is an exhortation to give alms to the indigent, although worded differently than other more direct exhortations (e.g., Q Ḍuḥā 93:10, and hadiths §1.221 and §6.67 in this volume). It warns that you will be punished if you ever refuse a mendicant; the only reason you may not be punished is if he lied about his need.

121 A reference to the Qur'anic verse «Let them laugh little and weep long, in recompense for what they have earned» ﴿فَلْيَضْحَكُواْ قَلِيلًا وَلْيَبْكُواْ كَثِيرًا جَزَآءً بِمَا كَانُواْ يَكْسِبُونَ﴾ (Q Tawbah 9:82).

122 I.e., if cattle were aware, as men are, of the certainty of death, they would be too fearful to eat; thus, humans should not live complacently, but rather, they should perform good deeds in preparation for the imminent end. R 513.

123 Lit. "only when earth fills his belly." R 514.

124 "Divine hadith" (Ar. *ḥadīth qudsī*) are words that issue from God and are reported by Muḥammad. They are distinguished from "prophetic hadith" (Ar. *ḥadīth nabawī*), which are Muḥammad's own sayings, and also from the Qur'an, as they may not be recited as part of the ritual-prayer.

125 This text is addressed to the prophet Moses. According to ʿAbd Allāh ibn al-ʿAbbās, Muḥammad said that "God spoke 140,000 hadiths to Moses, all in pious counsel." N 2:328.

126 Muḥammad is said to have uttered this prayer after reciting the Qur'anic verse «God then prompted the soul to immorality or to consciousness of him» ﴿فَأَلْهَمَهَا فُجُورَهَا وَتَقْوَاهَا﴾ (Q Shams 91:8). N 2:338.

127 Quraysh is the name of Muḥammad's tribe, who lived in Mecca and who were initially his bitter enemies.

Glossary of Names and Terms

ʿAbd al-Muṭṭalib patriarch of the Hāshim clan of Quraysh and the prophet Muḥammad's paternal grandfather.

Abraham (Ar. Ibrāhīm) a prophet in Islam, referred to frequently in the Qur'an, where he is said to have built the Kaaba, the "House of God" (Ar. Bayt Allāh), in Mecca. He is believed to be the forebear—through his son Ishmael (Ar. Ismāʿīl)—of the prophet Muḥammad.

Abū Hirr (d. 58/678) a companion of the prophet, more commonly known as Abū Hurayrah, who is reported to have narrated over five thousand hadiths.

ʿĀd an ancient Arabian tribe mentioned in the Qur'an. Its people rejected God's prophet Hūd and were consequently destroyed by a fierce, hot week-long wind.

Adam (Ar. Ādam) a prophet in Islam, the first human created by God. In the Qur'an, humankind is often referred to as "sons of Adam."

Age of Ignorance (Ar. jāhiliyyah) a term denoting the pre-Islamic period in which the inhabitants of the Arabian Peninsula were idol worshippers. The word "ignorance" in this term is usually interpreted as ignorance of the one true God.

Allies (Ar. anṣār) the people of Medina from the tribes of Aws and Khazraj who supported Muḥammad when he migrated there from Mecca. They are counted among the early companions.

alms-levy (Ar. zakāh or ṣadaqah) one of the "pillars" of Islamic practice, a mandatory duty for all Muslims. The annual levy on gold and silver is 2.5 percent.

Bilāl ibn Rabāḥ al-Ḥabashī (d. ca. 19/640) a companion of the prophet Muḥammad and one of the earliest converts to Islam. He was of Ethiopian origin, born into slavery in Mecca, and manumitted by Abū Bakr. He had a beautiful voice and served as Muḥammad's muezzin.

buried girl (Ar. maw'ūdah) a reference to the pre-Islamic practice of female infanticide condemned in the Qur'an (Q Takwīr 81:8–9).

children of Israel (Ar. banū Isrā'īl) the Jews, followers of the prophet Moses, referred to frequently in the Qur'an. Stories of the biblical prophets told by the Jews, the *Isrā'īliyyāt,* are usually frowned upon by medieval Muslim scholars as a source of Qur'anic exegesis.

collyrium or kohl (Ar. kuḥl) a powder used to darken the eyelids, both as cosmetic and salve, usually consisting of finely powdered antimony.

companions (Ar. aṣḥāb and ṣaḥābah) the men, women, and children who had direct personal contact with the prophet Muḥammad. As key figures in the early history of Islam, they are the first transmitters of the statements and deeds of the prophet.

confederates (Ar. aḥzāb) the name given to the Meccans and their combined Jewish and polytheist allies who came together to fight Muḥammad in Medina in 5/627 in the Battle of the Confederates. It was also called the Battle of the Trench (Ar. *khandaq*), after the trench dug around the city to prevent the Meccan forces from entering. After a fortnight, the siege was abandoned, and the failure of the Meccan expedition greatly strengthened Muḥammad's position in the Arabian Peninsula.

Dabūr the name of the west wind, said to blow away from—or have its back (Ar. *dubur*) to—the Kaaba. According to the Qur'an, it is the wind that destroyed the ancient Arabian tribe of ʿĀd.

dhimmī or ahl al-dhimmah (lit. "protected people") non-Muslims living in an Islamic state who pay dues and offer loyalty to the state in exchange for its protection and services. In the classical period the term refers primarily to Jews and Christians.

divine hadith (Ar. ḥadīth qudsī) hadiths which are believed to be God's direct speech. They are to be distinguished from regular prophetic hadith (Ar. *ḥadīth nabawī*), which are Muḥammad's own words, and also from the Qur'an. Unlike the Qur'an, divine hadith may not be recited as part of the ritual-prayer.

Emigrants (Ar. muhājirūn) those who migrated with Muḥammad to Mecca. Along with the Allies, they are revered by later Muslims for their service to Islam in its most difficult early years.

fasting (Ar. ṣawm) abstention from food, drink, and sex, from pre-dawn to sunset. Fasting during the month of Ramadan, the ninth month in the lunar Islamic calendar, is mandatory, but other optional fasts are also encouraged.

Friday prayer (Ar. ṣalāt al-jumʿah) the enjoined weekly congregational prayer, performed by Muslims at midday every Friday, usually in the main mosques of the city. It consists of listening to a two-part sermon and participating in a congregational ritual-prayer.

hadith (Ar. ḥadīth) or prophetic hadith (Ar. ḥadīth nabawī) often translated "traditions" of the prophet, these are reports of Muḥammad's words, deeds, and gestures. For Muslims, the corpus of hadiths holds a special position of authority and guidance, complementing the Qur'an.

hajj (Ar. ḥajj) the pilgrimage to Mecca mandated for every Muslim at least once in a lifetime. The hajj is performed in the month named for it, Dhu l-Hijjah, the twelfth in the Islamic lunar calendar. The hajj combines rituals performed by the prophet Abraham and the prophet Muḥammad.

Hallowed Spirit (Ar. rūḥ al-qudus) Qur'anic reference describing the archangel Gabriel (Ar. Jibrīl or Jibra'īl), who is also called the Spirit (*al-rūḥ*) and the Trustworthy Spirit (*al-rūḥ al-amīn*). He is said to have brought God's revelation to the prophets.

ḥanīf (pl. ḥunafā') a person who inclines to righteousness by following the monotheistic religion of the prophet Abraham. The relative adjective *ḥanīfiyyah* is used to refer to the religion of Abraham, and is often described as a precursor to Islam.

Hijrah Muḥammad's migration from Mecca to Medina in AD 622, which is considered the first Hijri year. The Islamic calendar begins from this date.

ḥudūd (sing. ḥadd) corporal penalties prescribed by Islamic law for certain major transgressions, notably murder, theft, adultery, drinking alcohol, and bearing false witness.

imam (lit. "leader") title of either the supreme leader of the Muslim community or an exemplary scholar or prayer-leader. In Shiʿi doctrine, the term denotes a man descended from the prophet Muḥammad through his daughter Fāṭimah and his son-in-law ʿAlī; for the Shiʿa, the imam is divinely guided and inherits Muḥammad's role of spiritual and temporal leadership.

Jesus (Ar. ʿĪsā) a prophet in Islam, referred to in fifteen different surahs and ninety-three verses in the Qur'an as the son of Mary, the Messiah (*al-Masīḥ*), the Word (*al-kalimah*) and the Spirit (*al-rūḥ*). In several hadiths, Jesus is also named as the true "Mahdī" who will come at the end of time and bring peace and justice to the world.

jihad (Ar. jihād) a righteous struggle against the forces of evil, the term can refer equally to battle with outside enemies or to combat one's own base nature.

Kaaba (Ar. Kaʿbah) a cubical structure in Mecca, the most famous sanctuary of Islam, and according to tradition built by the prophet Abraham. Muslims call it the house of God (Bayt Allāh): worshippers throughout the world face it in their daily prayer, and hundreds of thousands of pilgrims circumambulate it every year during the hajj and *ʿumrah* pilgrimages.

Khadījāh bint Khuwaylid (d. AD 619) a wealthy widow from the Asad clan of Quraysh, and the first wife of the prophet Muḥammad. Prior to their marriage, Khadījāh had employed Muḥammad as her trading agent. When Muḥammad received the call from God, she became the first Muslim, supporting him in the most difficult early years of his mission. She bore him two sons, who died in infancy, and four daughters, who lived to adulthood.

al-Mahdī (lit. "rightly guided one") the title of the restorer of religion and justice, who, according to a widely held Muslim belief, will rule before the end of the world.

Mary (Ar. Maryam) the mother of Jesus and the daughter of ʿImrān from the line of the prophet Abraham. She is accorded the highest status among women. A chapter of the Qur'an—Sūrat Maryam—is devoted to her.

Moses (Ar. Mūsā) a prophet in Islam, mentioned by name 136 times in the Qur'an, more than any other prophet. The Qur'an refers to his private conversations (*munājāt*) with God.

muezzin (Ar. mu'adhdhin) the person who recites the ritual call to prayer (*adhān*).

Noah (Ar. Nūḥ) a prophet in Islam. A chapter of the Qur'an—Sūrat Nūḥ—is devoted to him. In this surah as well as others, the Qur'an narrates the story of Noah's Ark.

qāḍī a judge.

quṣṣāṣ (sing. qāṣṣ) (lit. "tellers of tales") popular preachers who narrated stories of the prophets from the Qur'an, embellished with materials from other sources, including the so-called *Isrā'īliyyāt* from the Bible.

Qur'an (Ar. Qur'ān) the holy book of the Muslims, revealed by God to the prophet Muḥammad.

Quraysh the prophet's tribe. They lived in Mecca and were initially his bitter enemies, fighting him in the Battles of Badr, Uḥud, and Khandaq, where many were killed. When Muḥammad conquered Mecca in 8/630, they accepted Islam.

ritual-prayer (Ar. ṣalāh) the mandatory worship rite performed individually or in congregation five times a day by Muslims. It consists of prescribed sequences of bowings and prostrations to God, recitations of Qur'anic surahs, and supplications.

Ṣabā the name of the rain-bearing east wind that blows toward the Kaaba, apparently so called because it "yearns" (*taṣbū*) for the Kaaba.

salām (lit. "peace" and "well-being") term used by Muslims as a greeting.

Shiʿa (lit. "followers," the shortened form of *Shīʿat ʿAlī*, or "followers of ʿAlī") Muslims who believe that the prophet through divine revelation appointed ʿAlī to lead the Muslim community after him as imam and, as such, that ʿAlī was the rightful successor to Muḥammad in both his temporal and spiritual roles. Three major branches evolved: Twelver, Ismāʿīlī, and Zaydī.

sunnah (lit. "well-trodden path to a watering hole") refers to the accepted practice of pious forbears, and when used without qualifiers, usually to Muḥammad's practice.

Sunni (lit. "emulator of the prophet's practice") Muslims who believe that Muḥammad died without appointing an heir, and who revere the first four leaders of the community as "Rightly Guided Caliphs." The term "Sunni" emerged from the earlier, mainly political, appellation "people adhering to the sunnah and the majority group."

surah (Ar. sūrah) chapter divisions in the Qur'an. There are 114 surahs in the Qur'an, varying between 3 and 286 verses.

weighing scales (Ar. mīzān) symbolic rendering of divine justice on the day of judgment as an instrument that measures the good and bad deeds of humankind.

Yā-Sīn the name of the thirty-sixth surah of the Qur'an, and its opening word and verse. Some exegetes say it means "O human," while others say it is another proper name for the prophet Muḥammad.

Bibliography

Primary Sources

Abū Dā'ūd (d. 275/888). *Sunan*. Edited by Muḥammad Muḥyī l-Dīn ʿAbd al-Ḥamīd. 4 vols. Cairo: Dār Iḥyā' al-Turāth al-ʿArabī, 1970.

Abū l-Fidā', Ismāʿīl ibn ʿAlī (d. 672/1273). *Al-Mukhtaṣar fī akhbār al-bashar*. Constantinople, 1869.

Abū l-Saʿādāt, Asʿad ibn ʿAbd al-Qāhir al-Iṣbahānī (d. 634/1237). *Maṭlaʿ al-ṣabāḥatayn wa-majmaʿ al-faṣāḥatayn*. Tehran: Pizhūhishgāh-i ʿUlūm-i Insānī wa-Muṭālāʿāt-i Farhangī, 1385/1965.

ʿAlī ibn Abī Ṭālib (d. 40/661). *Ṣaḥīfat ʿAlī ibn Abī Ṭālib ʿan rasūl Allāh: dirāsah tawthīqiyyah fiqhiyyah*. Edited by Rifʿat Fawzī ʿAbd al-Muṭṭalib. Cairo: Dār al-Salām, 1986.

al-ʿAydarūsī, ʿAbd al-Qādir ibn Shaykh al-Hindī (d. 1037/1627). *Ta'rīkh al-nūr al-sāfir ʿan akhbār al-qarn al-ʿāshir*. Beirut: Dār al-Kutub al-ʿIlmiyyah, 1405/1985.

Bābī, Muḥammad ibn Mūsā (n.d.). *Sharḥ Shihāb al-akhbār*. MS. Princeton, NJ: Princeton University Library, Islamic Manuscripts, catalog no. Garrett 3402Y.

Baḥrānī, Yaḥyā ibn al-Ḥusayn (fl. 10th/16th c). *Shihāb al-ḥikmah dar ādāb wa-akhlāq wa-ḥikmat-i ʿamalī: mushtamil bar hazār wa-ṣad wa-bīst ḥadīth-i nabawī bi-īḍāḥ*. Edited by Muḥammad Ḥasan Zabarī Qayīnī. Mashhad: Majmaʿ al-Buḥūth al-Islāmiyyah, 2009.

al-Bukhārī (d. 256/870). *Al-Jāmiʿ al-ṣaḥīḥ*. Edited by Muṣṭafā Dīb al-Baghā. 7 vols. Damascus and Beirut: Dār Ibn Kathīr, 1987. Excerpts translated by Thomas Cleary in *The Wisdom of the Prophet: Sayings of Muhammad, Selections from the Hadith*, Boston: Shambhala Classics, 1994. Partial translation by Muhammad Asad as *Ṣaḥīḥ al-Bukhārī: Being the True Accounts of the Sayings and Doings of the Prophet Muḥammad*, Srinagar, 1935. Full translation by Muhammad Muhsin Khan as *The Translation of the Meanings of Sahih Bukhari*, Riyadh, 1997.

Catalog (Arabic) of the palace library of the Ottoman Sultan Bayezid II. Compiled by his royal librarian in 907/1502. MS. Budapest: Hungarian National Library, catalog no. Török F. 59.

al-Dhahabī (d. 748/1347). *Siyar aʿlām al-nubalā'*. 24 vols. Beirut: Mu'assasat al-Risālah, 2001.

———. *Ta'rīkh al-Islām wa-wafayāt mashāhīr al-a'lām*. Edited by 'Umar 'Abd al-Sallām Tadmurī. 53 vols. Beirut: Dār al-Kutub al-'Ilmiyyah, 1987.

al-Ḥabbāl, Ibrāhīm ibn Sa'īd (d. 482/1089). *Wafayāt qawm min al-Miṣriyyīn wa-nafar siwāhum*. Edited by Maḥmūd Ḥaddād. Riyadh: Dār al-'Āṣimah, 1987.

Ḥājjī Khalīfah (Kâtip Çelebi) (d. 1067/1657). *Kashf al-ẓunūn 'an asāmī l-kutub wa-l-funūn*. 2 vols. Beirut: Dār Iḥyā' al-Turāth al-'Arabī, 1941.

al-Ḥamawī, Yāqūt (d. 626/1229). *Mu'jam al-udabā' aw Irshād al-arīb ilā ma'rifat al-adīb*. 7 vols. Beirut: Dār al-Kutub al-'Ilmiyyah, 1991.

Hammām ibn Munabbih (d. 101/719). *Ṣaḥīfat Hammām ibn Munabbih*. Edited by Rif'at Fawzī 'Abd al-Muṭṭalib. Cairo: Maktabat al-Khānjī, 1985.

Ibn al-Abbār, Muḥammad ibn 'Abd Allāh (d. 658/1260). *Al-Takmilah li-Kitāb al-Ṣilah*. Vol. 1. Edited by Alfred Bel and M. Ben Cheneb. Algiers: Imprimerie Orientale Fontana Frères, 1920.

Ibn al-'Adīm, 'Umar ibn Aḥmad (d. 660/1262). *Bughyat al-ṭalab fī ta'rīkh Ḥalab*. Edited by Suhayl Zakkār. 11 vols. Damascus: Dār al-Fikr, 1988–89.

Ibn 'Asākir, 'Alī ibn al-Ḥasan (d. 571/1176). *Ta'rīkh madīnat Dimashq*. Edited by Muḥibb al-Dīn 'Umar ibn Gharāmah al-'Umarī. 80 vols. Beirut: Dār al-Fikr, 1995.

Ibn al-Athīr, Ḍiyā' al-Dīn (d. 636/1239). *Al-Mathal al-sā'ir fī adab al-kātib wa-l-shā'ir*. Edited by Muḥammad Muḥyī l-Dīn 'Abd al-Ḥamīd. 4 vols. Cairo: Muṣṭafā al-Bābī l-Ḥalabī, 1939.

Ibn 'Aṭiyyah al-Andalusī (d. 541/1147). *Fihrist Ibn 'Aṭiyyah*. Edited by Muḥammad Abū l-Ajfān and Muḥammad al-Zāhī. Beirut: Dār al-Gharb al-Islāmī, 1983.

Ibn Bābūyah, al-Ṣadūq al-Qummī (d. 381/991). *Man la yaḥḍuruhū l-faqīh*. Edited by Muḥammad Ja'far Shams al-Dīn. Beirut: Dār al-Ta'āruf, 1994.

Ibn Bashkuwāl, Khalaf ibn 'Abd al-Malik (d. 578/1183). *Kitāb al-Ṣilah fī ta'rīkh a'immat al-Andalus*. 2 vols. Cairo: al-Dār al-Miṣriyyah li-l-Ta'līf wa-l-Tarjamah, 1966.

Ibn Ḥajar al-'Asqalānī (d. 852/1449). *Fatḥ al-bārī bi-Sharḥ Ṣaḥīḥ al-Bukhārī*. Edited by Muḥibb al-Dīn al-Khaṭīb et al. 13 vols. Beirut: Dār al-Ma'rifah, 1980–89.

Ibn Ḥanbal (d. 241/855). *Musnad*. Edited by Aḥmad Muḥammad Shākir, Hāshim al-Ḥusaynī, and Aḥmad 'Umar Hāshim. 22 vols. Cairo: Dār al-Ma'ārif, 1949.

Ibn al-'Imād (d. 1089/1678). *Shadharāt al-dhahab fī akhbār man dhahab*. Edited by 'Abd al-Qādir al-Arna'ūt and Maḥmūd al-Arna'ūt. 10 vols. Damascus: Dār Ibn Kathīr, 1401/1981.

Ibn Isḥāq (d. ca. 150/767), in the recension of Ibn Hishām (d. 218/833). *Al-Sīrah al-nabawiyyah*. Edited by Aḥmad Ḥijāzī l-Saqqā. 4 parts in 2 vols. Cairo: Dār al-Turāth al-'Arabī, n.d. Translated by Alfred Guillaume as *The Life of Muhammad: A Translation of Ibn Isḥāq's Sīrat Rasūl Allāh*, London: Oxford University Press, 1955.

Ibn Khallikān (d. 681/1282). *Wafayāt al-a'yān*. 8 vols. Beirut: Dār al-Thaqāfah, n.d.

Ibn Mājah (d. 273/887). *Sunan*. Edited and translated into English by Muhammad Tufail Ansar as *Sunan ibn-i Mājah*. 5 vols. Lahore: Kazi Publication, 1993-1994.

Ibn Mākūlā, Abū Naṣr (d. 475/1082). *Kitāb al-Ikmāl fī rafʿ al-irtiyāb ʿan al-muʾtalif wa-l-mukhtalif min al-asmāʾ wa-l-kunā wa-l-ansāb*. 7 vols. Beirut: Dār al-Kutub al-ʿIlmiyyah, 1990.

Ibn Manẓūr (d. 711/1311). *Lisān al-ʿarab*. 15 vols. Beirut: Dār Ṣādir, 1955-1956.

Ibn al-Quḍāʿī, ʿAlī ibn Aḥmad (fl. ca. 5th/11th c.). *Tark al-iṭnāb fī Sharḥ al-Shihāb yā Mukhtaṣar-i faṣl al-khiṭāb*. Edited by Muḥammad Shīrwānī. Tehran: Tehran University Press, 1964.

Ibn Saʿd (d. 230/845). *Al-Ṭabaqāt al-kubrā*. Edited by Muḥammad ʿAbd al-Qādir ʿAṭā. 8 vols. + index. Beirut: Dār al-Kutub al-ʿIlmiyyah, 1997. Vols. 1 and 2 translated into English by S. Moinul Haq as *Ibn Saʿd's Kitab al-Tabaqat al-Kabir*, Karachi, 1967, 1972.

Ibn Shīrawayh, Shīrawayh ibn Shahradār (d. 509/1115). *Kitāb Firdaws al-akhbār bi-maʾthūr al-khiṭāb al-mukharraj ʿalā Kitāb al-Shihāb*. Edited by Fawwāz Aḥmad al-Zamirlī and Muḥammad al-Muʿtaṣim billāh al-Baghdādī. Beirut: Dār al-Kitāb al-ʿArabī, 1987.

Ibn Taghrī-Birdī (d. 874/1470). *Al-Nujūm al-zāhirah fī mulūk Miṣr wa-l-Qāhirah*. Edited by Muḥammad Ḥusayn Shams al-Dīn. 16 vols. Beirut: Dār al-Kutub al-ʿIlmiyyah, 1992.

Ibn Waḥshī, ʿAbd Allāh ibn Yaḥyā (d. 502/1109). *Sharḥ al-Shihāb*. MS. Madrid: Escorial Library, catalog no. 1382.

Ibn al-Warrāq, Yūsuf ibn Ibrāhīm (n.d.). *Taʿlīq ʿalā l-Shihāb*. MS. Tamegroute, Morocco: Dār al-Kutub al-Nāṣiriyyah.

al-ʿIrāqī, ʿAbd al-Raḥīm ibn al-Ḥusayn (d. 806/1403). *Risālah fī l-radd ʿalā l-Ṣāghānī fī īrādihī li-baʿḍ aḥādīth al-Shihāb li-l-Quḍāʿī*. Edited by Ḥamdī ʿAbd al-Majīd al-Salafī as an appendix to his edition of al-Quḍāʿī's *Musnad al-Shihāb*, 2:349–68. Beirut: Muʾassasat al-Risālah, 1986.

Ismāʿīl Pāshā (d. 1338/1920). *Hadiyyat al-ʿārifīn asmāʾ al-muʾallifīn wa-āthār al-muṣannifīn*. 2 vols. Istanbul: Milli Egitim Basimevi, 1951-1955.

al-Kulaynī, Muḥammad ibn Yaʿqūb (d. 329/940). *Al-Kāfī*. Edited by Muḥammad Riḍā Jaʿfarī. Translated by Muhammad Hasan al-Rizvani. Karachi: Khurasan Islamic Research Centre, 1978.

Mālik ibn Anas (d. 179/796). *Al-Muwaṭṭaʾ*. Edited by Muḥammad Fuʾād ʿAbd al-Bāqī. 2 vols. Cairo: Dār Iḥyāʾ al-Kutub al-ʿArabiyyah, 1951. Translated by Aisha Abdurrahman Bewley as *Al-Muwatta of Imam Malik ibn Anas: The First Formulation of Islamic Law*, London and New York: Kegan Paul International, 1989.

Maʿmar ibn Rāshid (d. 153/770). *Kitāb al-Maghāzī*. Edited and translated by Sean Anthony as *The Expeditions: An Early Biography of Muḥammad*. New York: New York University Press, Library of Arabic Literature, 2014.

al-Maqqarī, Aḥmad ibn Muḥammad (d. 1041/1632). *Nafḥ al-ṭīb fī ghuṣn Andalus al-raṭīb*. Edited by Iḥsān ʿAbbās. 8 vols. Beirut: Dār Ṣādir, 1388/1968.

al-Maqrīzī (d. 845/1441). *Ittiʿāẓ al-ḥunafāʾ bi-akhbār al-aʾimmah al-fāṭimiyyīn al-khulafāʾ*. Edited by Muḥammad Ḥilmī Muḥammad Aḥmad. 3 vols. Cairo: al-Majlis al-Aʿlā li-l-Shuʾūn al-Islāmiyyah Lajnat Iḥyāʾ al-Turāth al-Islāmī, 1971.

———. *Al-Khiṭaṭ al-Maqrīziyyah* (full title: *Kitāb al-Mawāʿiẓ wa-l-iʿtibār bi-dhikr al-khiṭaṭ wa-l-āthār*). 2 vols. Beirut: Dār Ṣādir, n.d.

———. *Kitāb al-Muqaffā al-kabīr*. Edited by Muḥammad al-Yaʿlāwī. 8 vols. Beirut: Dār al-Gharb al-Islāmī, 1991.

al-Munāwī, Muḥammad ʿAbd al-Raʾūf (d. 1031/1621). *Fayḍ al-qadīr Sharḥ al-Jāmiʿ al-ṣaghīr min aḥādīth al-bashīr al-nadhīr*. Edited by Aḥmad ʿAbd al-Salām. 6 vols. Beirut: Dār al-Kutub al-ʿIlmiyyah, 2006.

———. *Isʿāf al-ṭullāb bi-Sharḥ tartīb al-Shihāb*. MS. New Haven: Yale University, Beinecke Library, catalog no. Landberg 478; Cairo: al-Azhar University Library, catalog no. 307340.

Muslim ibn Ḥajjāj (d. 261/875). *Ṣaḥīḥ*. Edited by Muḥammad Fuʾād ʿAbd al-Bāqī. 5 vols. Cairo: Dār Iḥyāʾ al-Kutub al-ʿIlmiyyah, 2003. Translated by Abdul Hameed Siddiqui as *Sahih Muslim: Being Traditions of the Sayings and Doings of the Prophet Muhammad as Narrated by His Companions and Compiled under the Title al-Jamiʿ-us-sahih*, Lahore: Sh. Muhammad Ashraf, 1971-1975. Translated by Abu Tāhir Zubair ʿAli Zai and Nasiruddin Khattab et al. as *Sahih Muslim: English Translation of Sahîh Muslim*, Riyadh: Dār al-Salām, 2007.

al-Najāshī, Aḥmad ibn ʿAlī (d. 450/1058). *Rijāl al-Najāshī*. Edited by Muḥammad Jawād al-Naʿīnī. Beirut: Dār al-Aḍwāʾ, 1988.

al-Nasafī, Muḥammad Abū Ḥafs ʿUmar al-Māturīdī (d. 537/1142). *Sharḥ al-Shihāb ʿalā l-Nasafī*. MS. Nablus, Palestine: An-Najah National University (Jāmiʿat al-Najāḥ al-Waṭaniyyah), catalog no. 540.

al-Nasāʾī, Aḥmad ibn Shuʿayb (d. 303/915). *Kitāb al-Sunan al-kubrā*. Edited by Ḥasan ʿAbd al-Munʿim Shalabī. 12 vols. Beirut: Muʾassasat al-Risālah, 2001. Translated by Abu Tāhir Zubair ʿAli Zai, Nasiruddin Khattab, Huda Khattab, and Abū Khalīl as *Sunan An-Nasâʾi: English Translation of Sunan An-Nasâʾi*, Riyadh: Dār al-Salām, 2007.

al-Nawawī (d. 676/1277). *Al-Arbaʿūn ḥadith al-nabawiyyah*. Commentary by ʿAbd al-Majīd al-Shurnūbī l-Azharī. Cairo: Maktabat al-Qāhirah, 1970. Translated by Makrane Guezzou as *A Treasury of Hadith: A Commentary on Nawawi's Selection of Forty Prophetic Traditions*, Leicestershire, UK: Kube Publishing, 2014. Translated by Ezzeddin Ibrahim and Denys Johnson-Davies as *An-Nawawī's Forty Hadith: An Anthology of the Sayings of the Prophet Muhammad*, Cambridge: Islamic Texts Society, 1997.

———. *Riyāḍ al-ṣāliḥīn*. Edited by ʿAbd al-Azīz Rabāḥ and Aḥmad Yūsuf al-Daqqāq. Damascus: Dār al-Maʾmūn li-l-Turāth, 1976. Translated by Muhammad Zafrullah Khan as *Gardens of the Righteous: Riyadh as-Salihin of Imam Nawawi*, London: Curzon Press, 1975. Excerpts translated by Thomas Cleary in *The Wisdom of the Prophet: Sayings of Muhammad, Selections from the Hadith*, Boston: Shambhala Classics, 1994. Translated by M. Amin and A. Usamah bin Razduq as *Gardens of the Righteous*, Riyadh: Dār al-Salām, 1998.

———. *Sharḥ al-Nawawī alā Ṣaḥīḥ Muslim*. 18 vols. Beirut: Dār Iḥyāʾ al-Turāth al-ʿArabī, 1392/1972.

al-Qāḍī al-Nuʿmān (d. 363/974). *Daʿāʾim al-Islām wa-dhikr al-ḥalāl wa-l-ḥarām wa-l-qaḍāyā wa-l-aḥkām ʿan ahl bayt rasūl Allāh*. Edited by Asaf Ali Asghar Fyzee (Āṣaf ibn ʿAlī Aṣghar Fayḍī). 2 vols. Cairo: Dār al-Maʿārif, 1951. Translated by A. Fyzee and Ismail K. Poonawala as *The Pillars of Islam*, Delhi and Oxford: Oxford University Press, 2002-2004.

———. *Sharḥ al-akhbār fī faḍāʾil al-aʾimmah al-aṭhār*. Edited by Muḥammad al-Ḥusaynī l-Jalālī. 3 vols. Qom: Muʾassasat al-Nashr al-Islāmī, 1414/1993.

al-Qalʿī, al-Ḥusayn ibn ʿAbd Allāh (d. 629/1232). *Tartīb al-Shihāb ʿalā l-abjadiyyah al-maghribiyyah*. MS. Cairo: Dār al-Kutub, al-Khizānah al-Taymūriyyah, catalog no. 1889.

al-Qalqashandī (d. 821/1418). *Ṣubḥ al-aʿshā fī ṣināʿat al-inshā*. 15 vols. Cairo: Wizārat al-Thaqāfah al-Muʾassasat al-Miṣriyyah al-ʿĀmmah li-l-Taʾlīf wa-l-Tarjamah wa-l-Tibāʿah wa-l-Nashr, 1963.

al-Quḍāʿī, Muḥammad ibn Salāmah (d. 454/1062). *Daqāʾiq al-akhbār wa-ḥadāʾiq al-iʿtibār*. Istanbul: al-Maktabah al-ʿĀmirah, 1883.

———. *Dustūr maʿālim al-ḥikam wa-maʾthūr makārim al-shiyam min kalām Amīr al-Muʾminīn ʿAlī ibn Abī Ṭālib (karrama llāhu wajhahū)*. Edited and translated by Tahera Qutbuddin as *A Treasury of Virtues: Sayings, Sermons, and Teachings of ʿAlī*. New York: New York University Press, Library of Arabic Literature, 2013.

———. *Kitāb al-Inbāʾ ʿan al-anbiyāʾ wa-tawārīkh al-khulafāʾ wa-wilāyat al-umarāʾ*. Edited by ʿUmar Tadmurī. Beirut: al-Maktabah al-ʿAṣriyyah, 1999.

———. *Kitāb al-Shihāb*. Published in four trade editions: Istanbul: Uhuvvet Matbaasi, 1327/1909, with the title *Bin iki yüz hadis-i serif = Alf wa-miʾatān kalimah min ḥadith rasūl Allāh ṣalla Allah ʿalayhi wa-sallam: min al-ḥikmah fī al-waṣāyā wa-l-adab wa-l-mawāʿiẓ wa-l-amthāl*; Baghdad: Maṭbaʿat al-Shābandār, 1328/1910; Aleppo: al-Maṭbaʿah al-ʿIlmiyyah li-l-Shaykh Rāghib al-Ṭabbākh, 1354/1935; Morocco: al-Maṭbaʿah al-Mahdiyyah, lithograph, 1369/1950. Translated into French by René R. Khawam as *Le Flambeau ou les Sentences de Mouhammad, le Prophète*, Paris: Maisonneuve and Larose,

1991. Translated into Persian by Ḥamīd Farkhiyān, as *Shihāb al-akhbār*, Qom: Dār al-Ḥadīth, 1963.

———. *Musnad al-Shihāb*. Edited by Ḥamdī l-Salafī. 2 vols. Beirut: Mu'assasat al-Risālah, 1986. Edited by Ḥāmid 'Abd Allāh al-Maḥallāwī. Beirut: Dār al-Kutub al-'Ilmiyyah, 2011.

———. *'Uyūn al-ma'ārif wa-funūn akhbār al-khalā'if*. Edited by 'Abd al-Raḥmān 'Alī. Amman: Dār al-Yanābī', 1997.

al-Rāfi'ī, 'Abd al-Karīm ibn Muḥammad (d. 623/1226). *Al-Tadwīn fī akhbār Qazwīn*. Edited by 'Azīz Allāh al-'Aṭṭārīdī. 4 vols. Beirut: Dār al-Kutub al-'Ilmiyyah, 1987.

al-Rāwandī, Quṭb al-Dīn (d. 573/1178). *Diyā' al-shihāb fī Sharḥ Shihāb al-akhbār*, edited by Mahdī Sulaymānī l-Ashtiyānī. Qom: Dar al-Hadith, 1431/2010.

al-Ṣāghānī (OR: al-Ṣaghānī), al-Ḥasan ibn Muḥammad (d. 650/1252). *Al-Durr al-multaqaṭ fī tabayyun al-ghalaṭ wa-l-ḥukm 'alayhā bi-l-waḍ'*. Beirut: Dār al-Kutub al-'Ilmiyyah, 1985.

———. *Mashāriq al-anwār al-nabawiyyah 'alā ṣiḥāḥ al-akhbār al-muṣṭafawiyyah*, also titled *Al-Jam' bayn al-Ṣaḥīḥayn al-Bukhārī wa-Muslim*. Edited by Ashraf ibn 'Abd al-Maqṣūd. Beirut: Mu'assasat al-Kutub al-Thaqāfiyyah, 1989.

al-Sam'ānī, 'Abd al-Karīm ibn Abī Bakr al-Tamīmī (d. 562/1166). *Al-Ansāb*. Edited by 'Abd Allāh 'Umar al-Bārūdī. 5 vols. Beirut: Dār al-Fikr, 1998.

al-Sijilmāsī, Muḥammad ibn Manṣūr (fl. 7th c. H). *Sharḥ Shihāb al-Quḍā'ī wa-Sharḥ gharībihī*. Edited by 'Alī Najmī. 2 vols. Beirut: Dār Ibn Ḥazm, 2010.

al-Silafī, Abū Ṭāhir (d. 576/1180). *Mashyakhat al-shaykh al-ajall Abī 'Abd Allāh Muḥammad al-Rāzī*. N.d., n.p.

al-Subkī (d. 771/1370). *Ṭabaqāt al-Shāfi'iyyah al-kubrā*. 6 vols. Cairo: al-Maṭba'ah al-Ḥusayniyyah, [1906].

al-Ṭabarī (d. 310/923). *Ta'rīkh al-rusul wa-l-mulūk*. Edited by Muḥammad Abū l-Faḍl Ibrāhīm. 10 vols. Cairo: Dār al-Ma'ārif, 1977. Translated as *The History of al-Ṭabarī*, Ehsan Yarshater, gen. ed., Albany: State University of New York Press, 1987–1997, vols. 6–9. Vol. 6, *Muhammad at Mecca*, translated by W. Montgomery Watt and M. V. McDonald, 1987. Vol. 7, *The Foundation of the Community: Muhammad at Al-Madina A.D. 622–626/Hijrah–4 A.H.*, translated by W. Montgomery Watt and M. V. McDonald, 1987. Vol. 8, *The Victory of Islam: Muhammad at Medina A.D. 626–630/A.H. 5–8*, translated by Michael Fishbein, 1997. Vol. 9, *The Last Years of the Prophet: The Formation of the State A.D. 630–632/A.H. 8–11*, translated by Ismail K. Poonawala, 1988.

al-Tirmidhī (d. 279/892). *Sunan al-Tirmidhī (wa-huwa l-Jāmi' al-ṣaḥīḥ)*. Edited by 'Abd al-Wahhāb 'Abd al-Laṭīf. 5 vols. Medina: al-Maktabah al-Salafiyyah, 1965-1967.

al-Ṭūsī (d. 672/1273). *Ikhtiṣār ma'rifat al-rijāl*. Edited by Muḥammad Ṣādiq Baḥr al-'Ulūm. Najaf: al-Maktabah al-Ḥaydariyyah, 1961.

———. *Al-Istibṣār fī-mā-khtalafa min al-akhbār*. Edited by Muḥammad Mahdī Kharsān. Tehran: Dār al-Kutub al-Islāmiyyah, 1970.

———. *Tahdhīb al-Aḥkām fī sharḥ al-Muqniʿah li-l-Shaykh al-Mufīd*. Edited by Ḥasan al-Mūsawī Kharsān. Tehran: Dār al-Kutub al-Islāmiyyah, 1970.

al-Uqlīshī, Aḥmad ibn Maʿadd (d. 550/1155). *Al-Najm min kalām sayyid al-ʿarab wa-l-ʿajam*. Cairo: al-Maṭbaʿah al-Iʿlāmiyyah, 1302/1884. Reprint, Lexington, KY: University of Michigan Library Series, 2013.

al-Wāqidī (d. 207/822). *Kitāb al-Maghāzī*. Edited by Rizvi Faizer and translated by Rizvi Faizer, Amal Ismail, and AbdulKader Tayob as *The Life of Muḥammad: Al-Wāqidī's Kitāb al-Maghāzī*, London and New York: Routledge, 2011.

al-Yāfiʿī (d. 768/1367). *Mirʾāt al-jinān wa-ʿibrat al-yaqẓān*. 4 vols. Cairo: Dār al-Kitāb al-Islāmī, 1993.

Zakī, Khwājah Muḥammad (fl. ca. 6th/12th c). *Tarjumah wa-sharḥ-i Fārsī-i Shihāb al-akhbār*. Edited by Muḥammad Taqī Dānishpazhūh. Tehran: Intishārāt-i Dānishgāh-i Tihrān, 1349/1970.

Zayd ibn ʿAlī (d. 122/739). *Musnad al-Imām Zayd*, also known as *Al-Majmūʿ al-fiqhī*. Compiled by Abū Khālid al-Wāsiṭī (d. ca. 150/767). Beirut: Dār Maktabat al-Ḥayāt, 1966.

Secondary Sources

Abū Aḥmad, Ḥāmid. *Seminar notice on Kitāb al-Shihāb in Nādī l-Qiṣṣah, Cairo, Egypt, July 3, 2011*. Posted April 3, 2011. http://ahmedtoson.blogspot.com/2011/03/blog-post_04.html.

al-ʿAwnī, Ḥātim al-Sharīf. "Aḥādīth al-ḥikmah min *al-Shihāb*" [*Shihāb* lectures]. Filmed July 2–14, 2011. Sharjah, United Arab Emirates, 1:07:20. Posted October 2011. http://www.youtube.com/watch?v=oFKhJSbFJvw.

ʿAzzūzī, Muḥammad al-ʿArābī. *Qabas al-anwār wa-tadhlīl al-ṣiʿāb fī tartīb aḥādīth al-Shihāb*. Aleppo: al-Maṭbaʿah al-ʿIlmiyyah, 1935.

Brown, Jonathan A. C. *The Canonization of al-Bukhārī and Muslim: The Formation and Function of the Sunnī Ḥadīth Canon*. Leiden: Brill, 2007.

———. *Hadith: Muhammad's Legacy in the Medieval and Modern World*. London: Oneworld Publications, 2009.

Crone, Patricia. "What Do We Actually Know about Mohammed?" In *Open Democracy*, 10 June 2008. Accessed 12 August 2015. https://www.opendemocracy.net/faith-europe_islam/mohammed_3866.jsp.

Dīsī, Muḥammad ibn ʿAbd al-Raḥmān. *Tanwīr al-albāb bi-maʿānī al-Shihāb: taʿlīq ʿalā aḥādīth Kitāb al-Shihāb li-l-Quḍāʿī*. Beirut: Dār Ibn Ḥazm, 2013.

al-Dūmī, Ibn Badrān al-Ḥanbalī. *Sharḥ Kitāb al-Shihāb fī l-ḥikam wa-l-mawāʿiẓ wa-l-ādāb li-l-imām al-Quḍāʿī*. Edited by Nūr al-Dīn Ṭālib. 2 vols. Damascus and Beirut: Dār al-Nawādir, 2007.

Fitzpatrick, Coeli, and Adam Hani Walker, eds. *Muhammad in History, Thought, and Culture: An Encyclopedia of the Prophet of God*. 2 vols. Santa Barbara, CA: ABC-CLIO, 2014.

Garrett, Robert. *Descriptive Catalog of the Garrett Collection of Persian, Turkish and Indic Manuscripts Including Some Miniatures, in the Princeton University Library, by Mohamad E. Moghadam and Yahya Armajani, under the supervision of Philip K. Hitti*. Princeton, NJ: Princeton University Press; London: H. Milford, Oxford University Press, 1939.

al-Ghumārī, Aḥmad ibn Muḥammad. *Fatḥ al-wahhāb bi-takhrīj aḥādīth al-Shihāb*, edited by Ḥamdī ʿAbd al-Majīd al-Salafī. Beirut: ʿĀlam al-Kutub: Maktabat al-Nahḍah al-ʿArabiyyah, 1988.

———. *Al-Ishāb fī l-istikhrāj ʿalā Musnad al-Shihāb*. 2 vols. N.p., n.d.

———. *Munyat al-ṭullāb bi-takhrīj aḥādīth al-Shihāb*. N.p., n.d.

———. *Washy al-ihāb bi-l-mustakhraj ʿalā Musnad al-Shihāb*. 3 vols. N.p., n.d.

Goldziher, Ignaz. *Muhammedanische Studien*. Halle, Germany: S.M. Niemeyer, 1888-90.

Görke, Andreas, and Gregor Schoeler. *Die ältesten Berichte über das Leben Muhammads: Das Korpus Urwa ibn az-Zubair*. Princeton, NJ: Darwin Press, 2008.

Hamidullah, Muhammad. *The Life and Work of the Prophet of Islam*. Translated by Mahmood Ghazi and Mehmood Ahmed. Islamabad: Islamic Research Institute, 1998.

———, ed. *Majmūʿat al-wathāʾiq al-siyāsiyyah li-l-ʿahd al-nabawī wa-l-khilāfah al-rāshidah*. Beirut: Dār al-Irshād, 1969.

al-Ḥujūjī, Muḥammad ibn Muḥammad. *Minḥat al-wahhāb fī takhrīj aḥādīth al-Shihāb*. Edited by Hishām ibn Muḥammad Ḥayjar. Beirut: Dār al-Kutub al-ʿIlmiyyah, 2010.

Kamali, Mohammad Hashim. *A Textbook of Ḥadīth Studies: Authenticity, Compilation, Classification and Criticism of Ḥadīth*. Leicestershire, UK: The Islamic Foundation, 2005.

al-Kattānī, Muḥammad ibn Jaʿfar. *Jilāʾ al-niqāb ʿan aḥādīth al-Shihāb*. N.p., n.d.

———. *Al-Risālah al-Mustaṭrafah li-bayān mashhūr kutub al-sunnah al-musharrafah*. Damascus: Dār al-Fikr, 1964.

———. *Takhrīj aḥādīth al-Shihāb*. N.p., n.d.

Khalidi, Tarif. *Images of Muhammad: Narratives of the Prophet in Islam across the Centuries*. New York: Doubleday, 2009.

Kidwai, Abdur Raheem. *Daily Wisdom: Sayings of the Prophet Muhammad*. Markfield, UK: Kube Publishing, 2010.

Lane, Edward. *Arabic-English Lexicon*. Cambridge: Islamic Texts Society, 1984. First published 1863.

Lings, Martin. *Muhammad: His Life Based on the Earliest Sources*. Rochester, VT: Inner Traditions International, 1983.

al-Marāghī, Abū l-Wafā' Muṣṭafā. *Al-Lubāb fī sharḥ al-Shihāb*. Cairo: al-Majlis al-A'lā li-l-Shu'ūn al-Islāmiyyah, 1970.

McAuliffe, Jane Dammen, ed. "Hadith and Sunna." In *The Norton Anthology of World Religions: Islam*. New York and London: Norton, 2015, 166–95.

Motski, Harald, ed. *The Biography of Muhammad: The Issue of the Sources*. Leiden: Brill, 2000.

Motski, Harald. *The Origins of Islamic Jurisprudence: Meccan Fiqh before the Classical Schools*. Leiden: Brill, 2001.

Musa, Aisha Y. *Ḥadīth as Scripture: Discussions on the Authority of Prophetic Traditions in Islam*. New York: Palgrave Macmillan, 2008.

Qutbuddin, Tahera. "Muḥammad." In *Islam: A Short Guide to the Faith*, edited by Roger Allen and Shawkat M. Toorawa, 28–37. Grand Rapids, MI: Wm. B. Eerdmans Publishing Co., 2011.

Rubin, Uri, ed. *The Life of Muḥammad*. Brookfield, VT: Ashgate, 1998.

Sayf al-Dīn, Ṭāhir. *Risālah Ramaḍāniyyah: khazā'in imām al-muttaqīn*. Bombay: Ṭayyibī Da'wat Publications, 1372/1953.

———. *Risālah Ramaḍāniyyah: salsabīl ḥikam ghadaq*. Bombay: Ṭayyibī Da'wat Publications, 1364/1945.

Schacht, Joseph. *Origins of Muhammadan Jurisprudence*. Oxford: Clarendon Press, 1950.

Schoeler, Gregor. *The Biography of Muḥammad: Nature and Authenticity*. Edited by James Montgomery. Translated from German by Uwe Vagelpohl. Abingdon, Oxfordshire, UK: Routledge, 2001.

Ṣiddīqī, Muḥammad Zubayr. *Ḥadīth Literature: Its Origin, Development and Special Features*. Cambridge: Islamic Texts Society, 1993.

Sirāj al-Dīn, Ismā'īl, and Yūsuf Zaydān, eds. *Fihris makhṭūṭāt Dayr al-Iskūriyāl (Isbāniyā)*. Alexandria: Bibliotheca Alexandria, 2002.

al-Suhrawardy, Abdullah al-Mamun, trans. *The Sayings of Mohammad*. London: Archibald Constabel and Co., 1905.

Watt, William Montgomery. *Muhammad at Mecca*. Oxford: Clarendon Press, 1953.

———. *Muhammad at Medina*. Oxford: Clarendon Press, 1956.

al-Ziriklī, Khayr al-Dīn. *Al-A'lām: qāmūs tarājim li-ashhar al-rijāl wa-l-nisā' min al-'arab wa-l-musta'ribīn wa-l-mustashriqīn*, 3rd ed. 11 vols. N.p., n.d.

Websites

al-eman.com. Hadith search engine.

altafsir.com. Qur'an concordance and exegetical works.

alwaraq.net. *Al-Warrāq*. Arabic primary texts search engine.

baheth.info. *Al-Bāḥith al-ʿarabī*. Arabic lexicons search engine, including Ibn Manẓūr's *Lisān al-ʿarab*.

ejtaal.net. Arabic lexicons search engine, including Lane's *Lexicon* and Ibn Manẓūr's *Lisān al-ʿarab*.

hadith.al-islam.com. Hadith search engine.

islamic-books.org. *Rawḍat al-bāḥith*, Arabic primary texts search engine.

library.islamweb.net. Hadith search engine.

Index

abasement, §14.5
ʿAbd Allāh ibn al-ʿAbbās, 187n125
ʿAbd Allāh ibn ʿAbd al-Muṭṭalib, xiv
ʿAbd Allāh ibn Muḥammad, xiv
ʿAbd al-Muṭṭalib, xiv, §2.110, 181n55
ablution(s), §1.225, §3.12, §4.22, 183n79, 183n81. *See also* cleansing
Abraham (Ibrāhīm), xiv–xv, 185n102
absence, absent, xxxiii, §1.77, §2.99, §9.72, 186n117
Abū Bakr, xv
Abū Dāʾūd, xviii, xxii
Abū Hirr. *See* Abū Hurayrah
Abū Hurayrah, 182n66
Abū Lahab, xvi
Abū l-Saʿādāt, xxv
Abū Ṭālib, xiv, xvi
abundance, xiii–xiv, xli, §4.49
acceptance, §0.4, §7.87, 181n60
accommodating, §7.9, §§9.5–6
accountability, xv, §1.161
accumulation, §6.88
action, xv, xxiii, §3.38, §4.48, §6.44, §6.76, §6.86, 180n48, 182n72
acts, xxiii–xxiv, §1.1, §1.80, §2.75, §2.108, §2.110, §3.39, §4.48, §4.86, §§4.116–117, §9.29, 182n72, 183n83
ʿĀd, §3.5, 181n58
Adam (Ādam), xv; sons of, §1.238, §§3.40–41
adequate, §9.2, §9.25
adornment, §5.15, §16.10
adulation, §6.32
adultery, adulterer, §1.219, 179n42, 183n83
adversity, §7.71
advice, xvii, xx–xxiv, xxxviii, §0.3, §1.3, §1.10, §2.134, §3.34, §4.84, §4.104, §5.5, §5.25, §6.84, §9.59, §13.2, 187n125
advisor, §1.125, §5.25
affability, §1.153
affairs, xvii, §4.70, §4.79, §13.7
affection, xxiv, §1.21, §4.5, §4.29, §§4.35–36, §4.49, §5.30
affliction, §2.16, §2.22, §2.42, §2.126, §4.115, §6.49, §11.9, §16.12
affluence, xxxviii, §1.23, §1.9, §1.11, §1.32, §1.152, §1.214, §1.255, §1.257, §2.77, §3.25, §§3.34–36, §4.2, §4.56, §4.76, §4.90, §4.99, §§5.8–9, §§5.27–28, §5.32, §6.6, §6.24, §6.39, §7.14, §7.26, §7.41, §7.71, §7.73, §8.11, §9.7, §9.18, §§9.61–62, §13.3, §15.7, §16.2, §16.12, 177n10, 180n48, 181n60, 181n61, 183n86
afterlife, xv, xxiii, xxvii, §1.143, §§1.191–92, §1.235, §2.31, §2.59, §2.61, §2.107, §4.79, §4.88, §4.91, §7.82, §§7.94–95, §11.18, 178n27, 182n70
Age of Ignorance (*jāhiliyyah*), §1.45, 177n14, 179n42
aggression, xxiv, §1.132
aging, §1.22, 177n9
agriculture, 183n77

aid, xviii, §1.144, §2.101, §§3.4–5, 182n67
'Ā'ishah, 185n101
'Alī ibn Abī Ṭālib, xiv–xv, xvii, xxi, xxxi–xxxii, xxxiv, 184n87
Allies (*anṣār*), xvi, §1.184, 179n35
Almohads, xxvi
alms, almsgiving, §1.232, §1.236, §5.9, §5.13, §6.39, §7.76, §8.16, §9.7, 186n120
alms-levy (*zakāh* or *ṣadaqah*), xvii, xxiv, §1.209, §4.56, §§5.8, 178n16
ambiguity, xxxiv, §7.34, 179n38, 181n60
ambition, §2.65
'Amr ibn Umayyah, 182n64
amulets, §6.20
angel, §5.27
anger, xv, §1.86, §1.257, §2.7, §3.2, §3.21, §4.126, §8.12, §9.35, §9.56, §12.4, §16.4, 180n49
animal(s), §15.3
annihilation, §4.52
anṣār. *See* Allies
answer(s), xvii, xxi, xxiii, §1.248, §7.33, §9.72, §17.15
antimony, §9.21, 186n114
antisocial behavior, §6.7
anxiety, §5.33
apology, §6.86
appetite, §17.1
approachability, xxiv, §1.108
Arabia, Arabian Peninsula, xiii–xv, xvii, xxiii, xxxiv, xxxviii, 177n14, 181n58, 184n92
Arabic script, xxviii–xxxii
Arabs, §1.54, §1.230, 186n114
Ark, xv, §11.1
army, §1.212, §9.13; commander of, xvi, §1.125
arrogance, xiv, xxiv, §1.66, §1.256, §2.2, §2.53
arrows, §1.227
asceticism, xxxv, 180n48. *See also* rejection of the world
aspiration, §4.65
assembly. *See* gathering
assessment, xvii, xix, xxv, xxxix, §1.154, §1.164
astuteness, §1.107
al-'Atīq ('Amr) Mosque, xxviii
atonement, §1.70, §1.237, §8.5, 177n15
attack, §2.26, §2.86, §§17.9–10
audience, xxvi, §1.243, 180n49
authority, xiii, §2.62, §2.134
awe, §3.4, §9.57, §16.10, 180n45
Aws, xvi,
al-Azhar Mosque, xxvi, xxxix
al-'Azzūzī, xxv

baby, §7.119
bachelorhood, §6.16
Baghdad, xxvi
Baḥrānī, xxv
bane, §§1.58–68
banner, xvii, §1.133
baseness, 179n30
basin, 183n79
battle, §1.42, §16.7; for Conquest of Mecca, xvi, 184n92; of Badr, xvi, 181n58; of the Confederates (Aḥzāb), xvi, 181n58; of Khaybar, xvii; of the Trench (Khandaq), xvi; of Uḥud, xvi
beauty, §1.39, §1.64, §1.180, §1.224, §1.234, §2.118, §3.36, §6.90, §7.17, §7.54, §7.60, §16.10, §17.5, 180n45, 183n86, 185n98
beggar, §1.221, §1.256, §5.34, §6.67, §15.1

concealment, §1.232, §2.72, §2.102, §2.111, §2.116, §2.121, §§4.70–71, §5.20, §6.53, §9.49
conceit, xxiv, §1.64, §6.7
conciliation, §4.1, §8.10, §9.37
condiment, §9.64, §9.71
conditioning, §3.26
conduct. *See* behavior
congregation, §1.185, 179n33
Constantinople, xx
consultation, §6.8
consumption, §3.34, §7.52, §8.16, §10.6, 178n21, 183n83
contemptibility, §6.83
contentment, xxiv, §1.51, §3.37, §3.41, §4.12, §4.14, §9.33, 181n60
control, §8.12, 182n71
conversation, xiii, §1.25, §1.59
conviction, §1.129, §7.87, §9.10, §13.3
cooking pot, §7.57. *See also* pot
Copt, xiv
corporal penalties (*ḥudūd*), §4.86, 183n83. *See also* criminal act
correspondence, xxxiv, §2.92
corruption, §5.32
counsel. *See* advice
courage, xiii, xxiv, §1.62, §1.189, §1.231, §7.67, 181n52
covenant, §6.19
covetousness, §1.152, §6.81
cowardice, §1.231, §10.8
creator, xv, §0.1, 180n45
creature(s), xvii, §1.96, §2.106
criminal act, §4.86, 183n83. *See also* corporal penalties
crookedness, §11.13
crown, §1.54
cruelty, §3.26
crush, to, §5.32, §7.56
cunning, §1.6, §7.71
cure, §0.2, §1.17, §4.73, §5.17, §7.112, §17.3
curse(s), §1.258, §6.30, §§6.61–64
custodian, §1.236

Dabūr (West Wind), §3.5, 181n58
Daʿāʾim al-Islām (*Pillars of Islam*), xix, 179n34
Damascus, xxvii–xxviii, xxx, xl
damnation, §1.244, §1.257
Daqāʾiq al-akhbār wa-ḥadāʾiq al-iʿtibār (*Details of Reports and Gardens of Lessons*), xxi
Dār al-Kutub al-Ẓāhiriyyah, xxviii, xxx, xxxv
date-palms, §9.18, §9.60, §11.7
date(s), xxiii, §4.51, §4.100, §6.67, §7.67, §12.6, 183n78
daughter(s), xiv, §1.194, §2.123, 179n36
dawn, §4.50, 182n73, 183n79
day(s), §2.60, §2.90, §§2.95–97, §2.128, §2.132–133, §3.18, §4.103, §5.12, §6.21, §6.38, §6.91, §11.17, §14.7, 178n22, see also judgment day
dead, the, §1.45, §1.246, §3.34, §§6.63–64
deafness, §1.169
death, xiv–xv, xxviii, xxxvi, §1.48, §1.85, §1.88, §1.123, §1.137, §1.187, §1.195, §1.247, §1.261, §2.21, §2.83, §3.20, §3.34, §4.10, §4.45, §§4.90–91, §5.32, §§6.72–73, §7.23, §7.42, §7.76, §7.81, §7.103, §7.120, §8.5, §9.69, §10.4, §12.6, §13.2, §15.3, §15.7, §16.8, §17.16, 179n36, 186n119, 186n122; rattle, §7.70
debauchee, §8.2

mildness, §4.3
milk, §1.26, 177n11
mind, xxxiv, §7.67
mining, 183n77
miracle(s), xv
mirror(s), §1.104
miserliness. *See* stinginess
misfortune(s). *See* calamity
misleading, xix, §17.2, 179n38
mistake(s). *See* error
moderation, xxiv, §1.239, §1.257, §4.78, §5.1, §5.5, §7.10, 185n104
modesty, xxiv, §§1.55–56, §1.127, §1.166, §6.13, §7.39, §7.107
monasticism, §4.105
money, §2.125
morality, xvii, 177n11, 179n29. *See also* immorality
morning, §2.94, §15.8
Morocco, xxvi
Moses (Mūsā), xv, 187n125
mosque, xxviii, xxx, xxxix, §1.57, §2.104, §4.93, §4.120
Mosul, xxvii
mother(s), §1.43, §1.100, §2.87, 179n42, 183n81, 186n113. *See also* father(s), parents
moths, §7.97
Mount Ḥirā', xv
mouth, xviii, xxvi, §3.12, §7.53, §7.93, 182n75
mouthful, §1.114
al-Mu'ayyad al-Shīrāzī, xx
mudslingers, §6.75
muezzin, §§1.181–82, 179n34
Muḥammad, the prophet, as messenger, xiii, xv–xvii, xxxvi–xxxviii, §0.1, §0.3, §4.38, 179n42, 182n64, 182n72, 185n98, 186n124; as warner, xv, xxiv, xxxviii, §0.1, §1.261; ascension of, xv; companion(s) of, xvi, xviii, xxiv, §1.184, §4.82, §§11.2–3, 178n26, 179n35, 182n66, 183n85, 184n87, 184n92, 184n93, 187n127; family of, xiv–xvi, xviii, 181n55, 185n101; night journey of, xv; progeny of, xiv–xv, xxiv, §0.1, §4.83; sayings of, xiii, xv, xviii, xxiii, xxvii, 178n27, 179n36, 179n42, 181n52, 181n58, 182n64, 182n72, 184n97, 185n98, 186n116, 186n124, 187n125, 187n126. *See also* hadith
Muʿjam al-shuyūkh (*Compendium of Teachers*), xxii
al-Munāwī, xxv
murder, 183n83
Mūsā. *See* Moses
musk, xxiii, §9.70
Muslims, xiii–xiv, xvi–xix, xxv, xxxiv, §§1.134–40, §2.128, §2.134, §§4.13–14, §4.102, §5.25, §5.28, §6.37, §6.68, §7.74, §9.65, 178n18, 178n22, 178n25, 182n68, 184n91, 184n93, 185n100
Muslim (name), xviii, xxii, xxvi–xxvii, xxxviii
Musnad al-Imām Zayd (*Imam Zayd's Transmissions*), xix
Musnad al-Shihāb (*The Transmissions in the Blazing Star*), xiv, xxi, xxviii–xxx, xxxii–xxxv, xxxix–xli, 177n6, 186n116
mustache, §2.27, 181n52
al-Muwaṭṭā (*Leveled Ground*), xxvii

al-Naḍīr, xvi
naked, §14.4
nap. *See* sleep
al-Nasafī, xxiv

victory, §4.115
vinegar, xxiii, §9.64
virility, §1.147
virtue, xxi, xxiii, §1.11, §1.251, §2.135, §4.85, §5.25, §6.3, §6.56, §7.16, §7.62, §9.27, §9.43, §9.45, §11.14, 177n8, 184n90
visiting, xv, §4.5, §4.125, §7.91, §16.2, 185n101; the sick, §2.45, §4.88
vomit, §1.223

wages, xxiii, §1.132, §1.153, §3.31, §4.110, §6.58
warfare, §1.6
warning, xv, xxiv, xxxviii, §0.1§1.261, 186n120
waste, §1.65, §2.8, 183n78
water, xxix, §1.90, §4.66, §11.18, §12.3, §15.6, 182n75, 183n79, 183n81, 184n97; -carrier, §1.79
wavering, xv, §11.1, §16.8
wealth. *See* affluence
weapon(s), §1.117
weariness, §16.6
weeping. *See* tears
weighing scale, §1.165, §11.16
well-being, §6.60, §13.1, §17.14
wellsprings, §2.94
West, xvii, xxiv, xxvi, §7.85, 181n58
wheatstalk, §§11.7–8
whim(s), §0.2, §1.143, §1.257, §4.96, §7.96
wickedness, §1.12, §10.2
wife, §1.73, 179n42, 185n101; co-wife, 180n48
wind, §3.5, §11.8, §11.10, 181n58
wine, §§1.42–43
Winter, §1.116, §1.178, 178n22
wisdom, xxi–xxii, xxiv, xxvii, xxxviii, §§0.1–3, §1.31, §§1.37–38, §1.97, §1.120, §1.131, §1.186, §2.94, §3.35, §6.4, §7.2, §7.12, §14.3, 177n13, 178n23
wish, §1.143, §§2.16–18, §2.20, §§2.32–34, §2.37, §2.46, §2.59, §2.71, §2.84, §§2.120–21, §2.134, §4.13, §4.116, §4.129, §6.44, §6.72, §7.67, §7.91, §7.103, §12.2, 184n93, 186n119
wolves, §5.28
woman, women, xxxviii, §1.41, §1.73, §1.103, §1.210, §1.174, §1.224, §1.226, §1.228, §4.49, §§4.54–55, §4.121, §5.11, §6.28, §6.51, §6.80, §7.20, §7.88, §7.117, §9.19, §9.23, §9.26, §9.55, §11.13, 177n11, 178n25, 180n45, 182n65, 183n76, 183n86, 184n93, 184n94, 185n98, 185n101, 186n113, 186n118
womb, §1.69
wonder, §§3.19–23, 181n62
words, xiii, xv, xvii–xviii, xxi, xxiii, xxvii, xxxiii–xxxv, xxxviii, §§0.1–2, §1.38, §1.82, §1.99, §1.175, §1.238, §3.3, §3.36, §4.43, §6.92, §7.90, §7.107, §7.110, §8.10, §9.42, §9.67, 177n12, 177n13, 179n36, 181n58, 182n67, 183n83, 183n86, 185n99, 185n111, 186n120, 186n124
worker(s), xxiii, §4.110
world, xxiii–xxiv, xxvi–xxviii, xxx, xxxv, §1.119, §1.191, §1.216, §1.235, §1.254, §2.22, §2.59, §2.61, §2.78, §2.89, §2.91, §§2.99–100, §2.102, §2.107, §2.112, §2.116, §2.133, §3.20, §3.24, §§4.14–16, §4.62, §§4.78–79, §4.89, §§4.91–92, §4.115, §5.20, §5.26, §5.32, §6.49, §7.14, §7.27, §7.82, §§7.94–95, §7.102, §7.118, §7.122, §8.11, §9.26, §§11.17–18, §12.3,

About the NYU Abu Dhabi Institute

NYU
ABU DHABI
INSTITUTE

The Library of Arabic Literature is supported by a grant from the NYU Abu Dhabi Institute, a major hub of intellectual and creative activity and advanced research. The Institute hosts academic conferences, workshops, lectures, film series, performances, and other public programs directed both to audiences within the UAE and to the worldwide academic and research community. It is a center of the scholarly community for Abu Dhabi, bringing together faculty and researchers from institutions of higher learning throughout the region.

NYU Abu Dhabi, through the NYU Abu Dhabi Institute, is a world-class center of cutting-edge research, scholarship, and cultural activity. The Institute creates singular opportunities for leading researchers from across the arts, humanities, social sciences, sciences, engineering, and the professions to carry out creative scholarship and conduct research on issues of major disciplinary, multidisciplinary, and global significance.

About the Typefaces

The Arabic body text is set in DecoType Naskh, designed by Thomas Milo and Mirjam Somers, based on an analysis of five centuries of Ottoman manuscript practice. The exceptionally legible result is the first and only typeface in a style that fully implements the principles of script grammar (*qawāʿid al-khaṭṭ*).

The Arabic footnote text is set in DecoType Emiri, drawn by Mirjam Somers, based on the metal typeface in the naskh style that was cut for the 1924 Cairo edition of the Qurʾan.

Both Arabic typefaces in this series are controlled by a dedicated font layout engine. ACE, the Arabic Calligraphic Engine, invented by Peter Somers, Thomas Milo, and Mirjam Somers of DecoType, first operational in 1985, pioneered the principle followed by later smart font layout technologies such as OpenType, which is used for all other typefaces in this series.

The Arabic text was set with WinSoft Tasmeem, a sophisticated user interface for DecoType ACE inside Adobe InDesign. Tasmeem was conceived and created by Thomas Milo (DecoType) and Pascal Rubini (WinSoft) in 2005.

The English text is set in Adobe Text, a new and versatile text typeface family designed by Robert Slimbach for Western (Latin, Greek, Cyrillic) typesetting. Its workhorse qualities make it perfect for a wide variety of applications, especially for longer passages of text where legibility and economy are important. Adobe Text bridges the gap between calligraphic Renaissance types of the 15th and 16th centuries and high-contrast Modern styles of the 18th century, taking many of its design cues from early post-Renaissance Baroque transitional types cut by designers such as Christoffel van Dijck, Nicolaus Kis, and William Caslon. While grounded in classical form, Adobe Text is also a statement of contemporary utilitarian design, well suited to a wide variety of print and on-screen applications.

Titles Published by the Library of Arabic Literature

For more details on individual titles, visit www.libraryofarabicliterature.org

Classical Arabic Literature: A Library of Arabic Literature Anthology
Selected and translated by Geert Jan van Gelder

A Treasury of Virtues: Sayings, Sermons, and Teachings of ʿAlī, by al-Qāḍī al-Quḍāʿī, with the **One Hundred Proverbs** attributed to al-Jāḥiẓ
Edited and translated by Tahera Qutbuddin

The Epistle on Legal Theory, by al-Shāfiʿī
Edited and translated by Joseph E. Lowry

Leg over Leg, by Aḥmad Fāris al-Shidyāq
Edited and translated by Humphrey Davies

Virtues of the Imām Aḥmad ibn Ḥanbal, by Ibn al-Jawzī
Edited and translated by Michael Cooperson

The Epistle of Forgiveness, by Abū l-ʿAlāʾ al-Maʿarrī
Edited and translated by Geert Jan van Gelder and Gregor Schoeler

The Principles of Sufism, by ʿĀʾishah al-Bāʿūniyyah
Edited and translated by Th. Emil Homerin

The Expeditions: An Early Biography of Muḥammad, by Maʿmar ibn Rāshid
Edited and translated by Sean W. Anthony

Two Arabic Travel Books
Accounts of China and India, by Abū Zayd al-Sīrāfī
Edited and translated by Tim Mackintosh-Smith
Mission to the Volga, by Aḥmad ibn Faḍlān
Edited and translated by James Montgomery

Disagreements of the Jurists: A Manual of Islamic Legal Theory, by al-Qāḍī al-Nuʿmān
Edited and translated by Devin J. Stewart

Consorts of the Caliphs: Women and the Court of Baghdad, by Ibn al-Sāʿī
Edited by Shawkat M. Toorawa and translated by the Editors of the Library of Arabic Literature

What ʿĪsā ibn Hishām Told Us, by Muḥammad al-Muwayliḥī
Edited and translated by Roger Allen

The Life and Times of Abū Tammām, by Abū Bakr Muḥammad ibn Yaḥyā al-Ṣūlī
Edited and translated by Beatrice Gruendler

The Sword of Ambition: Bureaucratic Rivalry in Medieval Egypt, by ʿUthmān ibn Ibrāhīm al-Nābulusī
Edited and translated by Luke Yarbrough

Brains Confounded by the Ode of Abū Shādūf Expounded, by Yūsuf al-Shirbīnī
Edited and translated by Humphrey Davies

Light in the Heavens: Sayings of the Prophet Muḥammad, by al-Qāḍī al-Quḍāʿī
Edited and translated by Tahera Qutbuddin

Risible Rhymes, by Muḥammad ibn Maḥfūẓ al-Sanhūrī
Edited and translated by Humphrey Davies

A Hundred and One Nights
Edited and translated by Bruce Fudge

English-only Paperbacks

Leg over Leg: Volumes One and Two, by Aḥmad Fāris al-Shidyāq
Leg over Leg: Volumes Three and Four, by Aḥmad Fāris al-Shidyāq
The Expeditions: An Early Biography of Muḥammad, by Maʿmar ibn Rāshid
The Epistle on Legal Theory: A Translation of al-Shāfiʿī's Risālah, by al-Shāfiʿī
The Epistle of Forgiveness, by Abū l-ʿAlāʾ al-Maʿarrī
The Principles of Sufism, by ʿĀʾishah al-Bāʿūniyyah
A Treasury of Virtues: Sayings, Sermons and Teachings of ʿAlī, by al-Qāḍī al-Quḍāʿī with the **One Hundred Proverbs**, attributed to al-Jāḥiẓ
The Life of Ibn Ḥanbal, by Ibn al-Jawzī

About the Editor–Translator

Tahera Qutbuddin (Harvard University, Ph.D. 1999) is Associate Professor of Arabic Literature at the University of Chicago. She has also taught at Yale University and the University of Utah. After school in India, she studied Arabic language and literature in Cairo (Ain Shams University, B.A. 1988, Tamhīdī Magister 1990). Her scholarship focuses on intersections of the literary, the religious, and the political in classical Arabic poetry and prose. She is the author of *Al-Mu'ayyad al-Shīrāzī and Fatimid Daʿwa Poetry: A Case of Commitment in Classical Arabic Literature* (Leiden: Brill, 2005) and editor–translator of al-Qāḍī al-Quḍāʿī's *A Treasury of Virtues: Sayings, Sermons, and Teachings of ʿAlī* for the Library of Arabic Literature. Her current book project is *Classical Arabic Oratory: The Rhetoric and Politics of Public Address in the Islamic World*, for which she was awarded a fellowship by the Carnegie Corporation of New York and the American Council of Learned Societies. She has also published articles on the Qur'an, Muḥammad, the sermons of ʿAlī ibn Abī Ṭālib, Fatimid and Ṭayyibī literature, Arabic in India, and Islamic preaching.

www.ingramcontent.com/pod-product-compliance
Ingram Content Group UK Ltd.
Pitfield, Milton Keynes, MK11 3LW, UK
UKHW040130260225
455513UK00012B/81/J

9 781479 871469